The
CLASSIC
ALLOTMENT

No man but feels more of a man in the world if he have a bit of ground that he can call his own. However small it is on the surface, it is four thousand miles deep; and that is a very handsome property.

My Summer in a Garden, Charles Dudley Warner, 1829–1900.

THE

GENTLEMAN AND GARDENER'S

KALENDAR;

CONTAINING

Ample directions for the Cultivation of the Kitchen and Flower Garden, Green House, Nursery, Orchard, &c.

FOR THE

UNITED STATES OF AMERICA.

BY GRANT THORBURN,

SEEDSMAN AND FLORIST.

—••◆••—

THIRD EDITION, CORRECTED AND IMPROVED.

Price 50 Cents.

—••◆••—

NEW-YORK:

Printed by B. Young, No. 87 Nassau-street.

1821.

The CLASSIC ALLOTMENT

GORDON THORBURN

Pen & Sword Books Ltd
47 Church Street
Barnsley
South Yorkshire
S70 2AS

ISBN 978 1 84468 046 7

Printed and bound in Thailand
by Kyodo Printing Co (Singapore) Pte Ltd

Pen & Sword Books Ltd incorporates the imprints of
Pen & Sword Aviation, Pen & Sword Maritime, Pen & Sword Military,
Wharncliffe Local History, Pen & Sword Select, Pen & Sword Military Classics,
Leo Cooper, Remember When, Seaforth Publishing and Frontline Publishing

For a complete list of Pen & Sword titles please contact
PEN & SWORD BOOKS LIMITED
47 Church Street, Barnsley, South Yorkshire, S70 2AS, England
E-mail: enquiries@pen-and-sword.co.uk
Website: www.pen-and-sword.co.uk

Covers and special photography by Sarah Cuttle
Pictures on pages 19, 29, 58, 62, 73, 74, 81, 84, 90, 100, 107, 111, 118
courtesy of Thomas Etty Esq, seedsman

Acknowledgements

Many grateful thanks for help with pictures from allotment holders Emma Turner, Patty Hoskin, Jackie Cuttle, Micky Fisk, Debbie Longley and Anonymous of Laxfield, also from Ray Warner of Thomas Etty and David Kuzma, Special Collections and University Archives, Rutgers University, New Jersey.

The allotments featured are in Derbyshire, London, Norfolk, Suffolk and Wiltshire.

Contents

Introduction

There's little point rebelling against pesticide-coated, air-and-motorway-miled, flavour-free commercial fruit and veg if you then use the same kinds of killer powders and potions as the commercial growers.

Equally, there's little point in cherishing your own allotment if you plant those same tasteless commercial varieties you dislike buying in the supermarket.

If you're going to do it, do it properly. Don't spend a fortune at the garden centre on computerised propagators, solar-powered seed drills, Christmas potato barrels and electro-surgical weed removers. Away with all that modern flim-flam. Go green. Go basic. Go old fashioned. Go classical.

> We remember the fish, which we did eat in Egypt freely; the cucumbers and the melons, and the leeks, and the onions, and the garlick. But now our soul is dried away: there is nothing at all, beside this manna, before our eyes. And the manna was as coriander seed, and the colour thereof as the colour of bdellium.

> Numbers 11:5–7.

These words from the Old Testament describe events occurring sometime between 1600BC and 1200BC, but leeks and the rest were well known to the Egyptians long before then.

The plant now called Egyptian leek, or kurrat, a close relative of the ordinary leek, is grown throughout the Middle East for its leaves. Bdellium is a pearly-white healing resin extracted from trees of the genus *Balsamodendron*. Not a lot of people know that.

If you want to reach the Englishman's heart most quickly, just lean over the gate and praise his garden.

S P B Mais, first broadcaster of 'Letter from America', 1933.

A well-kept kitchen garden is at all seasons a delight to the eye. It has the same homely charm as a farmhouse kitchen, a home-made smock, or a team of horses ploughing.

Eleanor Sinclair Rohde, 1938.

Skirrets, Pea-Beans, Asparagus Peas, Scorzoneras, Cardoons, Silver Beet, Celeriac, Cocozelle Marrows, Chinese Artichokes, Couve Tronchuda, Pe-tsai, Pokeweed, Kohl-rabi, Parsnip-rooted Chervil, are all first-rate vegetables, but how many people have tasted them, let alone grown them?

Eleanor Sinclair Rohde, 1938.

Chapter One

Why Do It?

On your allotment now, in the Stone Age, and back again

Well, it's not the money. Growing your own vegetables, herbs and fruit the old-fashioned way will never satisfy the cost accountant even if you write off your time and labour. A financial adviser would say you were better making some extra cash by taking in washing or addressing envelopes and spending your wages at the supermarket.

Such a judgement misses the point by the vast distance that can only be attained by people who have a dried old prune instead of a soul. You cannot measure pleasure, excitement and satisfaction by any unit of length or breadth, neither can you count it nor write it down in a ledger. You work in that green allotment, for nothing, for several reasons. One is because it is much, much, much more pleasurable to dig up your own new potatoes, pick your broad beans and pull your carrots than it is to buy them in the shop. Two is because putting your time, effort and skill in place of agribusiness chemical sprays means that your produce will be unpolluted, more nutritious, and will taste much, much, much better – in truth, and in the extra flavour it gains from being all your own work.

There'll be a team of analytical chemists somewhere, all closely related to the aforesaid financial adviser, who will prove that the atomic composition of a shop potato is identical to that of your own, traditionally grown, allotment potato.

What utter nonsense.

One Sunday in early summer, with lunch coming up, you decide it's time to risk digging some roots from your potato rows. The first few flowers are starting to bud on your *Mr Little's Yetholm Gypsy*, a variety from the end of the nineteenth century.

You go to your potato patch with your fork. Your first Gypsies are smaller than new potatoes in the shop, and they seem skinless (they are, virtually) and shiny, and, would you believe it, red, white and blue. All you have to do is rinse the soil off them and throw them in some boiling water, biggest ones first.

They'll be ready in ten minutes. Don't put them on the table with the rest of the meal. Serve them on their own as a first course with butter, sea salt and the pepper grinder.

They'll look fantastic, everyone will ooh and aah, and you will never have tasted anything so delicious in all your born days.

This goes for everything else you grow yourself. It is always greatly superior in flavour, always fresher and therefore better nutritionally, always different and always more satisfying, and always not quite possible in any other way. In the shops they have vegetables that look more professional than yours. They are free from fluctuations. They are varieties that do not vary. They don't have scabby bits. The shopkeeper's lettuces don't have baby slugs in them. His *Romanesco* cauliflowers do not conceal caterpillars of hue identical to that of the vegetable in which they hide, and his carrots do not have networks of tiny canals artistically excavated by the maggots of the carrot fly.

Sometimes, your vegetables will have all these things, but yours are better. Far, far better. For a start they haven't been bathed twice a week in goodness knows what, but that isn't the only difference.

Consider a supermarket battery egg, probably three months old, versus one laid this very morning by your own free-grazing, free-scratching hen. Or think of an ordinary, bought birthday card against one hand-made for you by one of your small relations. That is the difference.

French beans, say, or purple sprouting broccoli, which need no preparation from the cook, go straight from the plant to the steamer and you can be eating them minutes from picking. Supermarkets can't match that. Supermarkets, even on their organic shelves, can't give you an everyday vegetable of such distinction that it is sufficient unto itself as a meal.

Steam some of your first purple broccoli shoots until they just soften and turn green. Let them cool for a wee while but not so as to go cold. Serve them, solo, warm, with mayonnaise. Absolutely wonderful.

This cannot be done any other way, because frozen broccoli has no distinction whatever, and fresh purple sprouting broccoli goes sad and floppy a day from picking. It has to be fresh from your plot.

So, where do we start?

My first garden was in south Norfolk. It was a huge square of grass with fruit trees around the edges. We had no money, I had no job, my dear wife went out to work, the possibility of starvation had to be offset somehow, so I started digging. I sought my father's opinion on where to site the vegetable plot, he being a farmer's son, and he said look where the grass grows the thickest and greenest and have it there. This was eminent common sense, so I mapped out a large T shape and began.

I read in a book what to do. You take the turf off a one-row width and barrow it around to wherever you are going to finish up. Then you take two spades' depth of soil out and barrow that around. Then you take the turf off the second row, put it upside down in the bottom of the first row-trench, then put two spades' depth of soil from the second row into the first, on top of the turf, and so on until you get to the end, when you will need your barrow loads to fill the last trench. I did this. It was hard work. If I had been more widely read, I might have followed instead the advice of Lawrence D Hills, godfather and archangel of the modern organic movement, who recommends piling up the turf for compost.

The first produce we had from that garden was turnip tops, young green thinnings, and they were as prized and thrilled over as any grown thing ever was. Now we were on our way. Now we were safe. We could grow our own food.

We were the nearest we have ever been to vegetarians, not through any imagined morality or matters of taste, but through necessity. One wouldn't advocate poverty as a desirable thing, but poverty with fresh vegetables of your own provides memorable treats in due season. Charles Lamb had something to say about this in 'Old China', one of the *Essays of Elia*, looking back from comfort to hard days.

> There was pleasure in eating strawberries, before they became quite common – in the first dish of peas, while they were yet dear – to have them for a nice supper, a treat. What treat can we have now? ... None but the poor can do it. I do not mean the veriest poor of all, but persons as we were, just above poverty.

Why do it? … Isn't it obvious?

When tradition began, and ended

For centuries, those persons in funds have been able to eat enough, and more than enough, of adequate diversity and delight, without producing any food themselves. Today, it is possible to eat well, at home, not only without growing or rearing anything, but without preparing and cooking anything.

You could go through your entire life and never peel a potato, break an egg or stuff a goose-neck with puy lentils and kochu chang. You don't even need to be able to recognise these things in their original state. In *The Importance of Being Earnest*, Lady Bracknell noted how fortunate she was never to have seen a spade. HM Queen Mary once exclaimed 'So *that's* what hay looks like!' In our modern world, anyone with an adequate income, regardless of social standing, need never know what a courgette looks like, or a Brussels sprout plant or, indeed, a *rossa lunga di Firenze*.

Your complete intake could be meals from every regional and national cuisine, consumed in front of your own television without benefit of chopping board, mixing bowl, saucepan or cookery book, much less benefit of spade, trowel, dibber and brushy hazel twigs. Of course, nothing's new under the sun. If you were the king, queen or similar in ancient times, you didn't do much cooking or gardening. There's nothing radical about a ready meal either. Colonel Sanders and Harry Ramsden can trace their lineage back at least as far as 1378AD, when you could go to the baker's shop and take away a whole chicken in a pie for eightpence, the equivalent of about £12 in today's money, or a roast thrush for a modern quid, which, compared to what you pay for a doner kebab, doesn't sound too bad.

Largely, though, there has been a transformation of late, from needing to understand all about your food and how to deal with it to not needing any knowledge or skills beyond being able to read a label.

At one time, if you were ordinary folk, your waking life was concentrated on food and if you didn't succeed in growing it, gathering it and/or catching it, you didn't get any. You had no choices; you took what was there and ate it. Now, in the developed world, we have so much food and so many choices that we have whole industries devoted to telling us what not to eat.

These industries flourish and burgeon despite the interesting fact that we are consuming more and more food with which we cannot interfere, and growing, buying and cooking fewer and fewer ingredients. Indeed, the less fresh food we bring into the kitchen, the more food gurus, celebrity cookery books and TV chefs we have thrust upon us.

Something must be done, but how far back should we go?

In the middle of the Stone Age, the transition was beginning from uncivilised life, defined as a society in which everybody is involved full time in getting food, to civilised life. Early or semi-civilisation is most people growing and rearing food full time but some smarter people doing other things, such as being rulers, priests and officials. Later,

THOUSANDS OF YEARS BG (BEFORE GARDENING)

Gardening and cooking are two highly advanced activities so closely related as to be inseparable. You can't enjoy much of your gardening success without cooking, but you can have cooking without gardening, and it was ever thus. Let us imagine for a moment that you are of an altogether different era, when only food mattered and the purpose of life was to survive. You're a young member of a Stone Age family, watching for the umpteenth time as your mother roasts a piece of meat over the fire. It's a rack of lamb – well, a lump of the ribcage of a rather elderly wild sheep that dad brought home the other day. You know that, no matter how hungry you are, the meat is going to take an awful lot of chewing. Flavoursome it will be, with lots of crispy outside bits of denatured protein, but there must be a better way, you think, to deal with tough old meat than quick-toasting it over a fierce fire.

Hmm. You absentmindedly tear off a piece of baked damper, made from broken wild oats and beech nuts, which is the nearest thing you have to bread, and make a salad wrap with some goosefoot/fat hen (*Chenopodium spp.*), chickweed (*Stellaria media*) and hogweed (*Heracleum sphondylium*) you gathered earlier. You had quite a good day today, coming home with wild raspberries as well, for afters.

Hmm. Again, you ponder. It is time that the art of cookery moved on a little. If only you had a cooking pot, you could simmer the meat until tender, but such an idea cannot occur to you because nobody understands how to work metal yet. You don't know anything about marinating in wine and other acidic fluids to help break down cellular structure. So you, the caveman equivalent of Heston Blumenthal, cook–scientist, must chew reflectively on your scraggy portion of leathery mutton, and wonder. Then, it hits you. You have The Idea.

Much to your family's amusement, you dig a circular pit about a stride in diameter, which you line with river clay and then with stones. It's hard work, with just pieces of flint for tools, but after a few days you have it and very neat it is. You carry water from the river in a leather bucket and fill your pit with it. You collect a mass of branches and build a big fire, into which you place some more stones, and ... Blast it. You hadn't thought of that. How are you going to get the hot, hot stones out of the fire and into the water? Using an early and soaking-wet form of oven glove, being a piece of the woolly skin of the old sheep in question, you manage to get some of the stones into the pit without burning yourself too much. Next time, you will build the fire nearer the pit, and you must turn your original mind towards the invention of tongs.

It is so gratifying when a new idea works, isn't it? Your family has gathered round now, to watch as your hot stones bring the water to a gentle boil. Perhaps they praise you for your discovery of the principle of the heat exchanger; perhaps not.

You throw pieces of meat into the simmering water. As the temperature falls, you put in more hot stones to bring it up again. This is great. Mother turns up with some oat-and-nut dough she was going to bake by the fire. She too has had an idea. Well, she is your mother, Heston. She throws lumps of the dough in with the meat. Your sister throws in some greenstuff she gathered, and a few roots of wild parsnip. Stew and dumplings. You have just invented stew and dumplings. Now, how do you get it out of the pit?

this would develop into full civilisation as we have come to know it, where hardly anybody grows or rears and almost everyone is a ruler, priest or official.

This process was made possible by the discovery that much better tools for hunting and farming could be manufactured out of metal. First it was copper, then copper fired with tin to make it harder as bronze, then iron.

In Scotland at this time, and other cold northern parts, life was still a sare ficht, but in the cradle of civilisation, the rich and warm lands of Mesopotamia where flowed the Tigris and the Euphrates, hindsight can spot early signs of civilisation's golden rule: the poor stay thin by doing all the manual work on an unsuitable diet, for thus the gods have ordered it, while the rich and idle get more and better food and so get fat. That was civilisation; things are different today. The gods have given up, so everyone in our post-civilised society can get more and worse food and get fat that way.

The basics of diet gradually changed in those metallic times, the Bronze and Iron Ages. More and improved fruits and vegetables were bred from their uncultivated ancestors. Bread, the staff of life, was made from superior grains. Cattle were domesticated, milked and put to work. Woodlands were managed, permanent settlements became usual, people stopped where they were and dug their gardens rather than roaming where the wild things were.

Stop roaming. Get digging. This allotment is waiting for improved fruits and vegetables.

All this happened everywhere in the Old World, but not simultaneously. While the Babylonians were lounging about in their olive groves, eating long lunches of roast lamb provided from their shepherded flocks and discussing the best recipes for the marvellous stuffing to be made from the mint, almonds and apricots in their gardens, the folk of the hard north were still nibbling on roots and chasing the wiry and wily forebears of the Soay and Herdwick sheep across the rocks. The Greeks, the Persians and the Egyptians had been through several stages of civilisation, including world wars (the world as they knew it), before anybody waved an iron carving knife in Britain. That was because of the weather and, for all you allotmenteers, it's still a problem, and it can be a very big problem depending on where you are gardening.

Pythias of Massalia visited Britain around 320BC and saw several varieties of grain growing in the south-east but commented on the lack of such multiplicity northwards. He sailed for six days to reach the land of Thule, where there was little corn, and what there was could hardly ripen in the inhospitable climate. Threshing had to be done indoors because of the rain.

Thule was more of a mythical place than a real one. Anywhere to the far north was Thule so, what with the rain and all, Pythias may have been talking about Shetland, the Hebrides, or possibly Lancashire. Wherever it was, it had no cultivated fruits and few domestic animals, so the brave, hardy and presumably very skinny Thulians ate millet, herbs, wild fruit and roots. When they did succeed with the corn, they went out to gather wild honey, started a brew and, a few days later, got sloshed on honey beer.

Pythias must have had it wrong about the millet. It surely wouldn't grow in Thule. He may have seen people gathering or even cultivating another of the grass family – the beaked or bottle sedge, *Carex rostrata*, or possibly the great pond sedge, *Carex riparia* – which look a bit like millet, are happy in the wet and, as well as edible roots, have small grain-like seeds which, *in extremis*, might justify the enormous amount of fiddling patience required to get yourself a decent quantity. Such hard, mind-numbing work may account for certain personality traits still extant in some parts of northern Britain.

Seakale grows wild, but even the ancient Britons probably didn't eat the leaves, which taste like iron filings mixed 50:50 with salt. Instead, they blanched the stems through sand and shingle, and you can do something similar. See page 102.

Wild sea beet, also called wild spinach and sea spinach, is the primordial beet. From it came all the beetroots, sugar beets, wurzels, chards, spinaches and so on. Some say that such refinement had a cost in flavour. Try growing it and see.

The Egyptians certainly had onions but probably not this one, despite the name.

Tree, Egyptian, or Bulb-bearing, Onion ($\frac{1}{12}$ natural size; detached bulblets, $\frac{1}{2}$ natural size).

The first gardener's lunch

In Scotland they call it 'piece'. In northern England it's 'bait', in Derbyshire 'pack-up', and almost everywhere it's 'snap'. Working men in pubs will discuss what she generally puts in my sandwiches and will tell tales of unrequested experimentation, unasked-for substitution of the old corned beef and pickle in buttered Mothers Pride with the new apple and date in low-fat spread Ryvita.

One such was a Roman ploughman called Simulus who, with no wife, was rather forced to make his own snap. A typical morning around 50BC is described in an anonymous poem, probably the earliest written description of a gardening man.

First thing, Simulus got his fire going again from last night, lit his oil lamp, and took a good handful of grain from his store. His quern was in the corner of his little hovel and there he sat by lamplight, grinding his corn while some water warmed in a pot on the fire. Satisfied with his flour, he kneaded it with the warm water into a firm dough.

There is no mention of him washing his hands so, as the late, great, Philip Harben said, if your hands are not clean before kneading dough, they will certainly be after. Anyway, our ploughman divided his dough into cakes, which he placed on the hearthstone.

He had no meat hanging that day. All he had was a lump of hard cheese. In the faintest light of dawn he went out into his garden, where he gathered four heads of garlic, some rue, and coriander in seed. These, with flakes of cheese and salt, he ground together with pestle and mortar, adding a little oil and vinegar and wiping the tears from his eyes. At last, he gathered all together into a ball.

This, his *moretum*, a Latin word sometimes translated as salad (food that has been salted) but really meaning something to bite into, with his chapati-bread fresh from the hearth, would be his midday meal, his ploughman's lunch. He had no nutritional knowledge beyond his own instincts and the folklore of the time, but, as a lunch, it was well enough balanced.

And so, his snap ready, he harnessed his oxen to the plough and went to work, perhaps dreaming of the day when he would be rich and eating lark's tongues steeped in red wine. Alas, it would be thirty or forty years before the Emperor Augustus Caesar introduced the lottery to Rome.

More likely, Simulus was thinking about what needed doing in his garden. He grew things to sell at market as well as to keep his own body and soul united. His herbs included dill, and rue, and elecampane (scabwort, wild sunflower), the roots of which were used as a digestif by over-indulgent townies and for veterinary purposes in the country, against skin sores. We probably wouldn't bother with rue nowadays because it tastes so awful.

His veg were cabbage, beet, lettuce, radishes, gourds, sorrel, endive, celery, rocket, and marsh mallow, whose young leaves made a fine salad and whose roots a delicate dish fried in butter. Mallows had a reputation as health givers, curers of all ills, possibly because of their purgative effect. He might have had a white, conical, root vegetable, a form of parsnip/carrot/skirret, developed through the parsley family, possibly the one we call turnip-rooted chervil, but most space would have been devoted to garlic, leeks and onions.

He had several varieties of onion. They were not the single-bulb, hot-flavoured onion we know, but rather of the bunching and heading sort. He had red shallots (*Allium ascalonicum*, the onion of Ashkelon also called scallion), and something like the white bunching leek/spring-onion we call ciboule or Welsh onion, by which we mean only that it is the foreign onion, not the onion from Wales.

Opposite: If only old Simulus had had an Aunt Kate, he could have made the most of his vegetables and been a legend in his own ploughman's lunchtime.

Making the Most of Vegetables

These simple recipes will give a delightful variety to the midday meal.

Carrots With Spaghetti.

2 carrots.
2 oz. dripping.
¼ lb. spaghetti.
Seasoning.
Boiling water.

Wash and brush the carrots in cold water, cutting off the green tops. Then scrape lightly and cut in fine shreds. Put them into a saucepan with enough boiling water to cover them, add salt to taste, and simmer slowly for 1 hour. Wash the spaghetti, break it in pieces, add to the carrots, and cook for ½ hour or until tender. Then drain thoroughly. Melt the dripping in the saucepan and brown slightly. Return the carrots and spaghetti and mix for a few minutes over the fire. Add seasoning to taste and serve very hot.

Geneva Vegetable Curry.

Some sliced onions.
1 teaspoonful flour.
Cold cooked vege-
    tables.
A chopped apple.
Boiled rice.
1 teaspoonful curry
    powder.
A little milk.
Dripping for frying.
A little desiccated
    cocoanut.

Melt the dripping in a saucepan and fry the onions and apple to a golden brown in it. Mix the curry powder, flour and milk to a cream. Now add enough boiling milk to make a cupful of the thickening. Then add it to the onions and simmer for 10 minutes. Add the cold vege-tables, cut in dice, and simmer for 20 minutes, stirring frequently. Sprinkle with the cocoanut and serve with a border of boiled rice.

Turnips With Potatoes.

2 teacupfuls cooked
    turnips.
2 oz. dripping.
Toast.
2 teacupfuls cooked
    potatoes.
4 tablespoonfuls hot
    milk.

Rub the potatoes and turnips through a wire sieve. Melt the dripping in a saucepan, add the sieved vegetables to it, and stir over the fire for a few minutes, seasoning to taste with salt and pepper. Then add the hot milk and beat the mixture until light and creamy. Arrange it neatly on a hot dish and garnish with toast cut in small triangles.

Mashed Haricot Beans.

1 cupful haricot beans.
1 tablespoonful butter.
1 teaspoonful chopped
    parsley.
2 tablespoonfuls milk.

Any remains of cooked beans may be used for this, but they must be very tender. Heat the milk first with a tablespoonful of butter or bacon fat, put the beans into this, and mash them with a fork until reduced to a pulp.

If the mixture is too thick a little more milk must be added. Season to taste, pile neatly in a vegetable dish, and sprinkle the chopped parsley over.

Rainbow Salad.

2 eggs.
1 beetroot.
1 turnip.
½ lettuce.
2 tomatoes.
1 tablespoonful grated
    carrot.
Cucumber.
Salad oil.

Shred the lettuce and place it in a glass bowl. Slice the beetroot, cucumber and tomatoes. Slice the prepared turnip and cut into pieces about the size of a shilling. Slice the eggs, which have been boiled hard. Place the eggs in the centre of the bowl, then put a ring of turnip round them. Then arrange a ring of cucumber slices, next grated carrot, then tomatoes and finish with a ring of beetroot, leaving the edges of the lettuce showing. Pour a little salad oil over the turnip and carrot before serving.

A POOR THING, BUT MINE OWN

Had there been television in 1850, Charles Elmé Francatelli, Chief Cook to Queen Victoria, would certainly have been on it. His message would have been about low-cost nutrition, at home rather than in school dinners, for the working masses. He would have been a big hit, perhaps the Jamie Oliver or Rick Stein of his day, because – if his books are anything to go by – he would have remembered something that modern recipe designers often forget. Mr Francatelli assumed that his readers, those people poor enough to have to do their own cooking, had common sense, common knowledge, and a certain liberty of soul.

Today's recipe follower, seeing specified 15 grams of dried squids' testicles (shouldn't that be tentacles? ed.), may send the nearest person out to Waitrose to get a 200-gram pack. Yesterday's, equipped with all the basic skills and using recipes only as a guide, would instead add an extra pinch of pepper, a splash of Worcester and some winter savory.

Our Victorian TV chef's recipe for Economical Vegetable Pottage could equally well be called Allotment Broth, and begins with a piece, as it were, to camera.

In France, and also in many parts of Europe, the poorer classes but very seldom taste meat in any form; the chief part of their scanty food consists of bread, vegetables, and more especially of their soup, which is mostly, if not entirely, made of vegetables.

And here it is, clearly aimed at the unbelievers.

If you are five or six in a family, put a three-gallon pot on the fire rather more than half full of water, add four ounces of butter, pepper and salt, and small sprigs of winter savory, thyme and parsley; and when this has boiled, throw in any portion or quantity, as may best suit your convenience, of such of the following vegetables as your garden can afford: any kind of cabbages cleaned and split, carrots, turnips, parsnips, broad beans, French beans, peas, broccoli, red cabbages, vegetable marrow, young potatoes, a few lettuces, some chervil, and a few sprigs of mint. Allow this to simmer by the side of the hob for two hours, and then, after taking up the more considerable portion of the whole vegetables on to a dish, eat one half, or as much as you may require, of the soup with bread in it, and make up your dinner with the whole vegetables and more bread. The remainder will serve for the next day.

Let me persuade you, my friends, to try and persevere in adopting this very desirable kind of food, when in your power, for your ordinary fare. I, of course, intend this remark more particularly for the consideration of such of my readers as are or may be located in the country, and who may have a little garden of their own.

A similar thing is given as Vegetable Porridge, this time featuring carrots, turnips, onions, celery and parsnips, parsley, chervil and thyme. You put it on the fire for two hours and then 'the whole must be rubbed through a colander with a wooden spoon, and afterwards put back into the pot and stirred over the fire, to make it hot for dinner'.

Hugh, Delia, Jamie, Rick, Nigella, Gordon – acknowledge the Master, Charles Francatelli, the greatest TV chef to exist before there was television.

What the Romans dug for us

If every fruit and vegetable said to have been brought to Britain by the Romans was actually so, we must have a great deal to thank the Romans for, and the poor old British tribes they conquered must have been living off brambles and acorns.

There was trade and contact with overseas peoples long before they invaded and, just as there were pre-Roman roads, some of the non-native vegetables and fruits must have been there ready for Julius Caesar to dine off. Cabbages, peas, asparagus, turnips, radishes, various members of the onion family, grapes, walnuts, cherries and more are all frequently described as introduced by the Romans.

In any case, to those British who were literally poor, Roman luxuries and exotica would have been impossible dreams. They'd be on the bean pottage and rough bread for most of the time, with the occasional meat broth possibly enriched with some of these newfangled onions, garlic, leeks and whatnot.

Ordinary meals during the day at the villa in Roman Britain would usually be cold and not so dissimilar to modern 'healthy eating', except it was all home grown, produced on the spot or locally traded. Bread, cheese, fruit, eggs and vegetables were the staples, with watered wine to drink. The beer favoured by the indigenous population was not considered suitable taking for Romans.

Dinner in the evening was the big occasion, worth the fire, fuel and best efforts of cooks and their enslaved skivvies, and special dinners with guests were very big indeed. Then the status-conscious host would wheel out the fatted dormice, the milk-fed snails, the roast suckling pigs and peacocks, every dish accompanied by its own complex sauce. What Roman cooks used to spice up the food would have any modern chef fainting in disbelief. Sauces were routinely made with a dozen ingredients or more, the objective seemingly being to prevent your dinner guests guessing what they were having, especially if the meat and fish were not at peak freshness (see Roman Relish, page 109).

Show-off dinner parties have never been expected to represent a healthy, balanced diet and, since large numbers of Romans and ancient Britons survived long enough to reproduce, we must assume that healthy eating of organic produce was what they mostly did, and it was reasonably easily achieved, then as now.

Did Alfred the Great have an allotment?

Time was when there were very few people in Britain and a great deal of land. In fact, relative to population there was so much land, most of it wooded, that there was no pressure on it. Folk could go and clear away some trees and scrub and cultivate to their hearts' content. They held the land in common and nobody thought there was anything wrong with that, or that there was any need to apportion the land or take it from the people who were, after all, only growing food and grazing a few animals.

If you could visit an Anglo-Saxon 'tithing' – from their word 'teotha', a tenth, meaning a small community of ten or so households – you would be impressed by the lack of fences. Apart from some enclosures in the village to keep young stock in, or to keep older stock out of orchards and gardens, there were none. The land around the village was worked by everyone, for everyone. They grew cereals – wheat, rye, barley and oats – and legumes – peas and beans. Every field had two years on and one year off, some land was managed as meadows, and the poorest parts were left to provide what they might, including coarse grazing and firewood. These rough bits have sometimes become what we now know as The Common. The good growing land has gone into ownership, and it was the Norman aristocrats who really began that process.

They liked owning land and they liked their new serfs, the Saxons, to work it for them. Bishops, abbots and so on felt the same way, but there was a problem. While Sir Humbert Fitzroy may have said he owned an area and so the soil of it, the essence of commonality of land was that Wulfstan and the Ældermen had ancient rights to the produce thereof, the right to graze, for instance, or to cut wood, or to take sand, gravel or turf. So, while the peat cutter (he with right of turbary) and the wood gatherer (he with right of estovers) could not enclose the land because they didn't own it, neither could the owner, because he'd be preventing the commoners from exercising their rights.

Well, that wouldn't do at all, so laws were passed allowing landlords to enclose, as long as they provided sufficient land with free use to compensate the commoners. And guess what. Landlords enclosed, but mostly didn't provide.

Organic gardening and the Battle of Bosworth Field

Let us roll forward to the fifteenth century and the house of a well-to-do merchant in a typical village. He would surely have had a garden. Only those urban masses, those foolish enough to be unblessed with riches while living in cities, did not have gardens. Such people were the Wars of the Roses' equivalent of the young mother who parks her jeep at Tesco, except they had no choice and no security of supply. They were in the hands of whoever happened to roll into the market place with whatever happened to be in season.

If you could, you grew. Our merchant's garden would have been tended by his wife and the servants. They had vegetables including onions, garlic and leeks, plus cabbages, which were then called worts, but, counting by numbers of species of plant, the majority crops were herbs, some culinary but mostly medicinal. Gardeners had to heal themselves in those days.

The culinary herbs would be the ones we know today and can buy dried in little glass jars, plus some we would regard as salad vegetables such as 'rokett', and some we would regard with a raised eyebrow. Bugloss we can understand – borage/comfrey family – but 'chykynweed'? You get quite enough chykynweed on your allotment without growing it on purpose.

One of the earliest gardening books, which came out in 1445 and covered the whole business of gardening without once referring to compost shredders, seed tapes, anything-icides, germinators or gas-powered weeding wands, listed only seventy-eight plants that were suitable for the gardener to grow. The great majority were herbs, to make remedies and to use in the kitchen to help get over the gustatory problems of half-rotten and/or salted meat, and well-travelled fish on Fridays. Besides the onion family and worts, the list includes radishes, lettuce and spinach, and that's it.

Other vegetables are mentioned in various early manuscripts but if we assume that the number of mentions corresponds roughly to their popularity and contribution to the common weal, 'parsenepys' and 'karettes' were what the seed merchants now call rare and unusual vegetables, the equivalent of scorzonera and cardoon.

For fruit, our merchant would have had apple trees, cherries and plums (bullace? damson? not Victoria, anyway) and possibly strawberries. As he was wealthy he could probably afford to buy imported dried fruit ('datys, fieggs and great raysyngs'). Being a countryman, he may well also have been a farmer in a small way. Nearly everybody in a village was. The main commercial crops would have been wheat, rye, peas and beans and some barley for brewing. Peas and beans would have been mainly for animal fodder and/or to feed those who could afford nothing else. Further north, the successful cereal crop was oats.

Everybody then was an organic good-lifer, everybody in the countryside anyway, which was most of the national population. In 1555 Sir Anthony Fitzherbert, presumably a descendant of the aforementioned Norman enclosers, described the job of good-lifing in his *Boke of Husbandrye*. These are his day-to-day instructions, presumably without tongue in cheek, to all good housewives (here translated into modern English for the benefit of today's good househusbands).

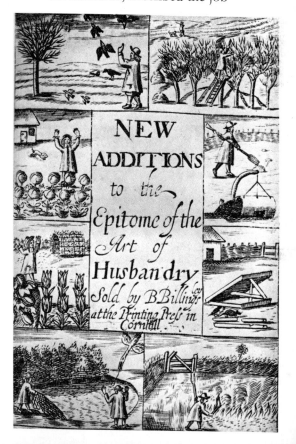

> First set all things in good order within the house, then milk the cows, see that the calves are suckling properly, strain the milk, grind corn and bake the bread, boil malt and brew the beer, make butter and cheese and feed the pigs twice daily. Every month there are particular things to do. In March, sow flax and hemp, to be weeded, harvested, soaked, spun and woven ...

Had enough? Fancy a takeaway from the Moti Mahal?

My vegetable love should grow
Vaster than empires, and more slow

The rise of England as a world power in the eighteenth century, with its attendant international trade and influx of foreigners, brought with it a greater variety of, and interest in, fruit and veg. The potato (taken to heart by the Irish but little thought of in England except as cattle feed), peas, beans, cauliflowers, celery – these rapidly became part of the national diet, supplied especially by a new phenomenon, the market garden.

It is perhaps hard for the modern reader, particularly anyone interested in allotment growing, to believe that vegetables were not eaten by large numbers of people 300 years ago. The main meals of the London poor mostly featured bread and hard cheese, with no vegetables and certainly no fruit, which was believed to be bad for you. Hard cheese, that token of ill luck and disinterest, was produced with what was left after the butter and proper cheese were made and the cream had gone to the rich man's table. Matured for years, it became almost indestructible:

> Those that made me were uncivil,
> They made me harder than the Devil.
> Knives won't cut me,
> Fire won't sweat me,
> Dogs bark at me but can't eat me.

Meat was a rarity for all the poorer people, and so the rural poor generally had a better diet with stuff from the garden. In northern towns they ate potatoes and porridge, which would have been much better than the fancy white but often adulterated bread those impoverished Londoners had.

In 1750, a tradesman with cash to spend in the city could get a dinner of boiled beef and carrots, beer and bread for tuppence ha'penny, about £18 in terms of average earnings at that time. Big dinners given at home by the wealthy, featuring all sorts of show-off dishes, did not feature carrots nor anything else so common. An often-cited Swiss traveller in England, Charles Moritz, complained that ordinary dinner was 'a piece of half-boiled or half-roasted meat, and a few cabbage leaves boiled in plain water, on which they pour a sauce made of flour and butter, the usual method of dressing vegetables in England.'

Ah but, things were about to change. The great and the good began to argue in favour of vegetables as a way of making meat go further. If only the poor people would realise it, they could be just as fit for work by doing without butter and the occasional treat of scrag-end of mutton. They should eat lentils instead. Here is a chap called Jonas Hanway, traveller, merchant, philanthropist and the first man in England to carry an umbrella, writing in about 1775.

With addition of legumens, roots and vegetables, five pounds weight of meat will go as far as we generally make ten or fifteen, and the consumer will be more free of scurvy.

Hanway's recipe for a stew or broth is excellent, although he's rather optimistic about it being enough for 'five stout men, or ten common persons including women and children.'

Lean beef 1lb
Split peas 1 pint
Potatoes 12oz
Ground rice 3oz
3 large leeks
2 heads celery
Water 9 pints
Salt

The nineteenth century at first saw little improvement in general nutrition – the poor didn't get enough of anything, never mind the right things, and the rich got too much – nor in the knowledge thereof. It was widely thought among the ruling classes that the Oliver Twists of the world would get very uppity if fed properly, and so it was bread, gruel and watery broth, and far too little of that, in the south and the big cities anyway. In other parts, where vegetables were more easily found, they were part of workhouse and prison diets.

Economising on institutional diets usually meant cutting out meat and potatoes, resulting a few months later in large numbers of inmates going down with scurvy and dysentery. When spuds went back on the list the diseases disappeared, but reintroducing mutton caused justices of the peace to express their sincere view that if you fed prisoners this way there would be an almighty crime wave. The poor would queue up to break the law so they could be found guilty and sentenced to live off the fat of the land.

Meanwhile, in 1847, a small assembly of vegetable zealots founded The Vegetarian Society of England. The French, who, as a matter of course, ate far more vegetables than the eccentric and barbarous English, thought such an idea hugely amusing and, for different reasons, it was. Vegetarianism as a way of life was even then an ancient notion but it had nothing to do with sensitivity towards animals or with food economics and sustainability. It was based in the belief that eating animals brings out the beast in the eater and was therefore prejudicial to high civilisation. Fine minds thinking fine thoughts could only be compromised by bacon sandwiches and steak pies, plus there was disgust at the hoggish excesses in which some high earners indulged, flaunting their loadsamoney with feasts of suckling pig and roast peacock.

However, there was a significant difference between now and then. In the mid nineteenth century, both vegetarianism and gluttony were the preserve of the wealthy

IN AN ENGLISH COUNTRY GARDEN

How many kinds of ved-jer-tubbles grow, in an English country, ga-ha-den? Having inexplicably missed onions out of his allotment broth, Mr Francatelli corrected himself in his recipe for jugged hare, which again begins with a piece to camera. Read it aloud, in the manner of Nigella Lawson.

> It does sometimes happen that when you are living in the country, in the neighbourhood of considerate gentlefolks who possess game preserves, that they now and then make presents of a hare and a few rabbits to the poor cottagers in their vicinity. And when you are so fortunate as to have a hare given to you, this is the way to cook it. First, cut the hare up into pieces of equal size ...

Hey, wait. Sorry, Chef, but you have already lost most modern Cooks Aspirant. You have assumed that the poor cottager in question knows about hanging his hare in a cool, dry place for a few days, depending on the weather, then skinning it and drawing it or, as Mrs Hannah Glasse instructed in her book *The Art of Cookery Made Plain and Easy* in 1747, casing it, which is to say taking off the case.

The joke about 'First catch your hare', so often and wrongly attributed to Mrs Glasse and even Mrs Beaton, is much older than that, possibly thirteenth century. Proverbially, it's similar to 'Don't count your chickens until they are hatched.'

So, if we go to the butcher and get a hare ready cut, what else do we need for the pot, Chef? Carrots and onions from the allotment, nearly three pints of water, flour to thicken (could use left-over mashed potato, Chef), allspice, salt and pepper, and, of course, Francatelli's favourite, winter savory. Modern jugged hare for the wealthier cottagers among us may include a good half-bottle of port.

and educated. While the poor ate whatever they could get, only those who could afford excess could choose to forego it. Thus it was a small proportion of society who could feel, like the poet Shelley, healthy and virtuous through becoming vegetarian, rather than being prone to disease, superstition and crime, like all meat eaters.

One thing that was as true then as now was that a lot of disease and bodily malfunction was due to bad diet, especially lack of fruit and veg. The mistake made then, when food science was non-existent, vitamins were undiscovered and transmission of disease was poorly understood, was to attribute all the malaises of humankind to the same cause. There was plenty of proof that switching from big, meat-dominated dinners to a light diet, including fruit and veg, had an almost instant effect on weight and health, and so the conclusion was that one would be even better off if all one ate was fruit and veg.

Vegetarians who ate milk and eggs were getting, without knowing it, the benefits of meat eating without eating the meat. They had a well-balanced diet, with all the protein,

FORCE OF HABIT; OR, CITY SUSPICIONS

'Arry (who is foraging for his camping party). "**Look here, my good woman, are these cabbages fresh?**"

In the person of artist J C Walshe, Mr Punch – the paparazzo of his day – espies a young gent at a market garden on the outskirts of London, circa 1890.

vitamins, minerals and so on that are essential to the human. Vegetarian evangelists who forswore every food except fruit and veg ran into trouble, because they had no real idea of how to get around the difficulties.

By the end of the Victorian era, the national diet had not improved. A survey of the poor in Leeds in 1902 showed that half the children had rickets. Another survey in 1904 found that almost all poor children subsisted on white bread, jam and tea and a third of them didn't even get that. The British army reduced its minimum height qualification to five feet and still rejected forty per cent of applicants as unfit for service.

In our public schools the concern was to fill the children with cheap stodge so, during term time anyway, the rich kids were little better off nutritionally than their poor counterparts. There were a few beacons of enlightenment, such as Christ's Hospital school where, in 1901, vegetables including potatoes, peas, lettuce and cabbage were fed to the inmates.

Elsewhere, usually behind four walls, the gardeners to the gentry were fulfilling their obligations, to provide vegetables and fruit the year around. Here was gardening, without modern science, being brought to its peak of achievement.

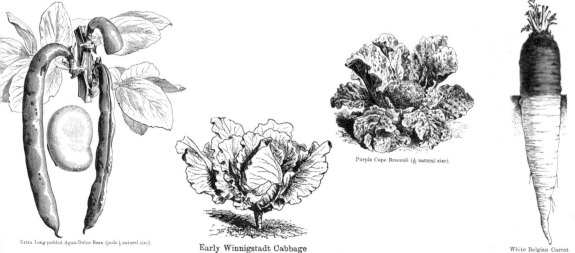

Extra Long-podded Agua-Dulce Bean (pods ⅓ natural size).

Early Winnigstadt Cabbage
(1/12 natural size).

Purple Cape Broccoli (1/10 natural size).

White Belgian Carrot
(⅓ natural size).

When marketing meant shopping

Butter	Pollywolly low-fat grease made out of water, additives, caustic soda and rapeseed oil
Milk	Skimmed milk
Bread	Bread
Bacon	Low-fat sausages
Beef	Frozen lasagne
Chicken	Chicken nuggets
Fish	Frozen prawn vindaloo
Sprouts	Frozen peas
Cauliflower	Baked beans
Potatoes	Oven chips
Cabbage	Spaghetti hoops
Sugar, apples (for a pie)	Low-fat desserts, crisps, biscuits, ice cream
Jam	Chocolate spread
Marmalade	Fruit corners

The column on the left is a shopping list taken from a 1928 issue of *Good Housekeeping*, which in turn is based on a nutritional needs table worked out by a government committee during the First World War. The full version gives quantities per day for the family. The beef and chicken are alternatives, and it recommends that the bacon fat and extra apple should be given to the children. A good part of this list could be self-produced from the allotment rather than bought in the shops.

The column on the right is an estimate of what some modern fridge, freezer and microwave owning families might buy instead. Except for the peas and your own version of baked beans, none of it could be allotment produced. (Yes, you could rear chickens, but you wouldn't make nuggets.) Easy question: which list makes the better diet?

Whose fault is it?

Early domestic refrigerators cost twice as much as a car; the first one in the UK was bought in 1924. Later models could poison you if they leaked their compressor gas, sulphur dioxide. By the 1930s they were safe but still expensive; by the 1950s they were in common use in the UK among middle-class families; by the 1960s almost everybody had one and houses were not built with pantries any more.

As the fridge became widespread so 'doing the marketing', that is the daily food shopping, declined. Not for the only time in our history, a rise in convenience led eventually to a fall in quality, and the point of no return came one day in the 1970s when a refrigerated van called at a branch of Marks & Spencer to deliver some trays of fresh-cream trifles, made ready to eat by Northern Foods. That was the day the new shop-bought ready meal revolution began.

Until that day, it had been universally believed that any ready-to-eat food bought in a shop was inferior to its equivalent made at home. A shop-bought cake was nothing like as good as the one mother made, nor a pie, nor the potted meat, nor anything that was the shopkeeper's. The purchase of same implied laziness at the least, and possibly moral turpitude in any housewife seen doing it frequently.

Today, not only are the best-quality ready-meals as good as mother ever made: some of them are better. Did your mother know how to make an equally fine lamb jalfraisi and a raised pork pie and a boeuf Bourguignonne and a nasi goreng and a saltimbocca?

Probably not. But whatever the ready mealers do, no matter how hard and long they try, they can't beat you and your allotment at fresh fruit and veg. It was always so, and always will be.

FOOD OF LATE YEARS

... is dressed in Masquerade, seasoned with slow Poisons, and every Dish pregnant with nothing, but the Seeds of Diseases both chronick and acute. Poor and Rich live as if they were a different Species of Beings from their Ancestors, and observe a Regimen of Diet, calculated not to supply the Wants of Nature, but to oppress her Faculties, disturb her Operations, and load her with, till now, unheard of Maladies.

Robert Campbell, *The London Tradesman*, 1747

Allotments allotted

By the sixteenth and seventeenth centuries, the gentry were full pelt at tidying things up, enclosing common land and taking it unto themselves, occasionally giving the poor folk thus dispossessed small parcels of land to cultivate around their tied cottages. The great majority of those folk, the working people of Britain, were agricultural. They worked on the land and to an extent lived off it but, as that changed with the rise of industry and migration to the cities, living off the land became impossible for many. Various Acts of Parliament, such as the General Enclosure Act of 1845, made provision for pieces of land to be allotted for use by the poor but, generally, more powerful interests prevailed. Allotment holders might find their gardens were required for building houses as the cities grew, and that was that.

In 1887, Parliament passed the Allotments and Cottage Gardens Compensation for Crops Act, which was the first step towards modern allotment keeping in that it obliged

local authorities to provide land for allotments if people wanted them. Guess what … again, the authorities mostly didn't bother, so several more Acts were passed strengthening the law.

The Act of 1908 produced a great surge in allotment holding and there were almost 59,000 allotments by the end of 1909 in England and Wales, but not many in Scotland and Ireland. The privations of the First World War made food growing an emergency. Land was confiscated from its owners and by 1920 there were 1,330,000 allotments, a figure which could only go down as the war was over and there was no security of tenure.

A drastic reduction was followed by a recovery, when allotments were made a measure to help the unemployed in the recession of the early 1930s. Numbers rose again to over 600,000, plus 80,000 railway allotments, followed by a gentle fall due to demand for building land, followed by a massive upsurge during the Second World War and the Dig for Victory campaign. At the peak, there were 1,750,000 allotments, the most there had ever been and, almost certainly, the most there ever will be.

Today's number is not known exactly; it's probably between 250,000 and 300,000, and provision versus demand varies tremendously, like so many things, according to the luck of the postcode. Where there are waiting lists for allotments, local authorities must take account of and plan for such demand, and consider it, and form an opinion on it, and define what, under the circumstances, a sufficiency of allotments might be. They may, by agreement, purchase or lease land, whether situated within or without their boroughs, districts or parishes. Unfortunately, when push comes to budget, they are not actually forced to do anything.

Here we see how the privations of the First World War made food growing an emergency.

Is yours an allotment, or isn't it?

No, it isn't. An 'allotment' (1922 Act) is any parcel of land, whether attached to a cottage or not, of two acres or less, held by a tenant under a landlord and cultivated as a farm or garden, or partly as a farm and partly as a garden.

An 'allotment garden' (1922 Act) does not exceed a quarter of an acre (forty perches) and is wholly or mainly cultivated by the occupier for the production of vegetable or fruit crops for consumption by himself or his family. Or his family? So, he doesn't have to eat it himself, but he can't sell it.

HORTICULTURE

... is both an art and a science. It is an art in that through practice certain skills are developed in necessary operations ... essential to successful culture. It is a science in that underlying these practices is an orderly array of fundamental facts which explain and direct their performance.

Encyclopaedia Britannica, circa 1935.

The Act of 1950 did away with farm allotments, confirmed that all allotments were allotment gardens, and allowed the keeping of hens and rabbits in addition to growing veg and fruit. There is no given size but custom and practice dictate that the British Standard Allotment is 1/16 of an acre, 10 perches, about 300 square yards or, if you must, about 250 square metres.

Chapter Two

And So, To Begin

That was all very interesting, but what about your allotment? What's to do?

Well, you can get your simple remedies from the chemist, so you don't need rows and rows of medicinal herbs taking up time and allotment space. Even given that freedom, most people will still not have enough room to grow everything they'd like, and as many hours as they might like to spend pottering around. Choices will have to be made. To help, we shall try to tell you the cons as well as the pros of each crop and offer you the most direct route to the right choices and, thence, to success.

By 'success' we mean having those gourmet experiences described above, and having enough of most of the vegetables and fruit you decide that you want.

Our kind of allotment gardening means getting pleasure and satisfaction at a level you select yourself, without getting involved in a lot of marginal mystique and fiddle-faddle and, above all, without regular recourse to proprietary powders, miracle potions and fancy inventions. Unless disaster strikes, we shall purchase nothing from that fantastic array of packets, bottles and life-easing devices on the shelf at the garden

It's not for the sake of a ribboned coat, or the ten pence prize money, or the glory. It's just that you want to beat everybody else on the allotments.

centre. Alas, this may mean us not winning the big cup for most points at the produce show, although we can hope to get some First in Class prizes by accident. Nor shall we have total success in every instance for everything we do. Even the big seed companies have crop failures, so we are bound to.

Mistakes will be made, important tasks will be forgotten. We shall leave undone those things that we ought to have done. The weather will beat us sometimes, but, mostly, things will be all right. If one crop does badly, generally another will do exceptionally well, and we shall try to use the minimum of mental and physical effort. It is still quite a lot of effort, but it is the minimum.

AMAZE YOUR FRIENDS

You have large tomatoes, sage, chives, land cress and lettuce from the allotment? All you need is some soft cheese and you can make Bird's Nest Salad, the very apogee of refinement in *hors d'œuvres* for the Modern Housewife of 1925.

Chop finely some sage leaves and chives, mix with the soft cheese and roll into ovoids about the size of a sparrow's egg. If you've never seen a sparrow's egg, think mint imperials. Cut the toms in half, scoop out the seeds and insert two or three of your eggs instead. Arrange some lettuce leaves and cress on a posh plate, maybe some cucumber too, artfully distribute the tomato nests, present to your guests with a French dressing and accept the applause graciously.

The beginning

... is not what tools you need, nor how to double-dig and rake your patch to the finest of tilths. It isn't crop rotation or how to prick out aubergine seedlings.

The beginning is deciding what you want to grow. The size of your allotment will have an influence on this; so will its location. If you live many feet above sea level where there are only three frost-free months in a year, there is no future in deciding that you want to grow outdoor Italian plum tomatoes, sweetcorn in rainbow colours or clever-dick little spherical cucumbers. A great deal of effort would be required for you to beat the climate.

In fact, most summer vegetables require twelve to sixteen weeks from sowing to picking. Your correspondent at one time lived in the upper Eden valley in Westmorland where the last frost can be in early June and the first in mid September, so you can see the problems. On the other hand, being where he was, he never had to do any watering.

If you live in a warm, dry part, don't bother with cauliflowers, beetroots, kohl rabi and swedes unless your water is not on a meter and you have an irrigation system, such as a slave willing to empty lots of watering cans every evening.

ALLOTMENT SUSHI

What's the main thing about a platter of sushi? It looks nice. What else (apart from the small portions)? Well, if you push the emperor's new clothes to one side and find yourself saying that one kind of raw fish tastes very like another kind, it's the stuffings and dips that make it.

A platter of your own vegetables with stuffings, dressings and dips can look as good as any sushi and have a much more satisfying variety of flavours. So, get slicing, into matchsticks, ovals, shreds, florets, whatever. You won't have all of these available at once, of course, but you'll have some of the vegetables some of the time, and maybe some that aren't on the list.

Raw: carrot, celery, courgette, cucumber, leek, lettuce and other leaves, onion, pea, pepper, tomato.

Blanched: bring to a rolling boil, count to ten, drain and refresh in cold water: broad bean, broccoli, cauliflower, French bean, mangetout, red cabbage, runner bean, swede, turnip.

Blanched and dressed: some white veg will tend to discolour even after blanching, so toss these also in lemon juice or French dressing: celeriac, kohl rabi, Jerusalem artichoke, salsify, scorzonera.

Cooked: beetroot, haricot or any seed beans.

Half-cook some cabbage leaves – Savoy or January King types are best for this – after chopping out the thick stem parts. Make some savoury stuffing, spread on the leaves, roll up, chill and slice into little Swiss-roll logs. This is also excellent with the larger leaves from spinach beet or Swiss chard; just lightly steam them first.

Dips and sauces: 'Hoy you' sauce, very like Hoisin sauce, is made by placing equal quantities of soy sauce and damson jam in a pan, heating gently and stirring until the two combine, and allowing to cool. Variations on the theme such as 'Who, me?' sauce, 'Who's in?' sauce, 'Blimey what's this?' sauce, *et cetera*, are made by using light instead of dark soy, other jams or jellies, and adding various quantities of fresh or dried chilli and finely sliced spring onion. Crab apple jelly and light soy make a delightful 'Oh my' sauce, while dark soy and blackberry jelly with chopped fresh chillies make 'Oh wow' sauce.

Allotment sushi presupposes a visit to the oriental stores. Thin slices of well-blanched swede dressed with oyster sauce are very good. A good base for a dip is a fifty-fifty mixture of soy sauce and either dry sherry or wine vinegar. Another goody is two parts Thai fish sauce (*nam pla*) with one part lemon or lime juice and one part wine vinegar. To these bases add some things from your allotment: crushed garlic, grated onion, sliced spring onion, grated horseradish, grated ordinary radish, sliced chillies, chopped herbs, chopped tomato. If you don't have chillies buy some ginger root. Add sugar to taste.

When choosing what to grow, you might like to have something there to pick most of the year, or you might want to go for a few crops that are ready together, to feed the freezer and other tools of preservation. You might not want to bother with commodity crops like onions, and go instead for delicacies like mangetout, frilly red lettuce and twenty-seven sorts of Szechuan radish. And so on. As each vegetable and fruit is described in this book, the difficulties as well as the advantages will be shown up so you don't set off on Mission Unlikely.

There will be information about the main enemy or enemies of each crop and how to beat them if you want or need to.

If a task is necessary, it will be included. If it is unnecessary, it will not. If a vegetable is difficult to grow out of proportion to its desirability or likelihood of success, such facts will be stated.

You will not be offered a long list of possible varieties. The main traditional, old-fashioned ones will be recommended; if you want to go for F1 hybrids and other new strains, fair enough, but remember most of them were not really developed for small-scale you.

The doubts of seed

Seed merchants are probably more steely eyed than they used to be, employing extra accountants, webmasters and suchlike to help them maximise their whatever it is, but you might think the profession of seedsman can have only limited potential for modernisation. It has to remain basically sound with long roots reaching far into the past. Honest types of humankind with straw hats and grubby aprons must labour long over their task of plant improvement and generation, their finger-ends gently transmitting green magic.

'Fraid not. The truth is that commercial and bureaucratic pressures are taking the variety out of varieties. Traditional varieties were bred by selection, by carefully watching how certain characteristics repeated themselves in certain strains and trying to make the best use of those observations to improve matters. That is largely true still, but then the work was done by gardeners for gardeners of all types: cottage, allotment, market, walled, and farmers too.

Many of the varieties in the modern seed catalogue have been developed not for gardeners but by scientists for large-scale commercial farmers serving the large-scale supermarkets.

Classical allotmenteers are not interested in cultivation using a tractor that costs the same as a Rolls Royce, harvesting on a given day by a picking, sorting and washing machine costing ditto and transporting crops by 40-ton truck and aeroplane, nor are we out to make 100-yard chilled displays of regular perfection and conformity. So why are we expected to grow fruit and veg of varieties that meet these priorities so foreign to us?

New varieties are often not really new, and they're rarely interesting. They are mostly progressions of the same few dominant commercial breeds, the only ones which can justify going through expensive EC testing programmes. What's that got to do with our allotments? So, when choosing your seeds, beware.

The seedsman's chief marketing tool remains the seed catalogue and its website equivalent. It is a work of deceit or, at least, a masterpiece of truth economy. It's not the words you can read that are important; it's the words you can't read because they are not there.

If, for example, a description of a vegetable variety doesn't specifically mention flavour, then you can be sure that the vegetable in question has none. If taste is mentioned as outstanding, you must scrutinise the rest of the text for signs of a trade-off because there are no perfect vegetables. Desirable qualities such as bumper yield, magnificent flavour, beauty, reliability and resistance to allotment perils do not, as a rule, all occur together.

In the commercial world, demand is for varieties that offer symmetry, toughness in transit, bright colour, ease of harvesting by mechanical means and, of course, heavy cropping. Flavour is not the top priority and it may not even be a consideration. Many of the traditional gardeners' varieties are much nicer to eat but you can get canker on your inelegant, two-pronged parsnips, your impatient sprouts may fluff out like little green roses and your turnips sometimes turn up with all the prime characteristics of an oak bed-knob.

Anyway, here you are, sitting in your fireside armchair in late autumn looking at the seed catalogue or, perhaps, mousing your way through the websites in your winter lunch hour. You dream of those year-turned days when the sap riseth, the bullock starteth and springeth the wood new, and you faileth to start the rotavator. Take care. Do not be seduced. Read between the lines.

Fleshy pods, stringless, and of fine flavour. Compact plants make it ideal for growing under protection.

Translation: *Compact plants* – 'The main stem of this dwarf French bean variety is shorter than its pods, so they hang on the ground and get covered in soil. Slugs also appreciate the fine flavour and find the fleshy pods easy to reach and bite into.' ... *ideal for growing under protection* – 'If you haven't got them under cloches and the temperature falls a half degree below the average for July, all your plants will wither and die immediately.'

Very quick maturing. Large pure white curds.

Translation: 'This totally flavourless cauliflower variety was developed for farmers who need to book the harvesters in advance. It will stand around doing nothing for weeks then, at 8.30am on a Tuesday, the whole row will reveal heads the size of footballs. You pick one, shading your eyes from its snowy brilliance. You make cauliflower cheese for supper, deep-fried florets with a dip for the jumble-sale committee lunch, a gallon of cauliflower soup for the freezer, and you finish the blasted thing with white sauce and a gammon steak on Thursday. On Friday when you go in the allotment, all the other forty-seven heads are wide open, going brown and infested with caterpillars.'

Courgette F1 Orelia 10 seeds, £1.99. Broccoli Nine Star Perennial 150 seeds, £1.99. Marjoram 2000 seeds, £1.55. Lovage 125 seeds, £1.55. Leek Lyon Prizetaker 500 seeds, £1.20.

Seed merchants, who have always been the nicest possible and most genuine people, have this serious blind spot. They like to set their packet prices around the assumption that the same gardener who wants to grow only 10 plants of yellow courgettes will also want 500 leeks, not to mention 2,000 marjoram plants 'needing warmth and full sun for the flavour to develop. Useful in pasta sauces and pizza.'

While you are working out how spending £1.55 on some seeds, followed by a good summer, could force you into setting up an Italian restaurant, think also of 125 lovage plants. Your correspondent is experienced in lovage. Three plants make a forest in which giraffes could hide. The scale implicit in 125 plants is Amazonian, and you haven't yet considered your 150 permanent broccoli trees.

Not that it is so simple. If you plant ten courgette seeds, only seven will come up. Of those, two plants will be spindly and useless, and so you will have five, one of which will die after planting out, leaving you with the probability of enough courgettes for a small family provided the weather is kind – sunny, not too dry, with lots of insects to pollinate the flowers. If it's a cold, horribly wet growing season you will be eating your own courgettes just once this year. Most of your pathetic crop will rot when no bigger than a toddler's todger, except for one, which will become a three-foot, ten-pound banana-coloured marrow while you are away for a weekend.

When you sow your 500 leek seeds, they will all come up. If you give them enough room and look after them, they will all make good leek plants, so you have something like ten times as many as any normal, leekophile family would want.

It seems you must have too few seeds, or too many, or far, far too many even for people who don't think 500 is too many. In a packet of lettuce seeds, there are so many you couldn't count them, and they all come up, too. No family, unless it kept sheep, could deal with that many lettuces. No family, unless it had a six-acre garden (or ninety-six allotments) and the whole of spring and early summer off work, would have the room to grow them and the time to transplant all the little baby lettuces.

At one extreme, you are supposed to want 1,300 Lobjoits Cos, each growing to 40cm long, weighing a kilo and originally costing you approximately 0.0838461 per cent of the price of a cos lettuce in the shop. At the other extreme, for the same price as your 1,300 lettuce seeds, you can get two seeds of F1 Apache 'patio type' chilli super-pepper. Nobody wants just two, so you have to pay for a packet with six in, costing the same as 1,300 lettuce, 500 leek and 400 summer cabbage altogether.

THE POETRY OF SALAD

The Reverend Sydney Smith, 1771–1845, among his many essays, pamphlets and humorous stories, penned a poem describing his favourite dressing for lettuce. Uniquely, your correspondent believes, and with compassion and consideration, the recipe is here presented as an abstract, thus sparing the reader from the poetry.

Pass two boiled potatoes [presumably peeled] through a sieve or mouli. Add one teaspoon of mustard powder, two of salt, four of olive oil and two of vinegar. Mix with the pounded yolks of two hard-boiled eggs and a little grated onion, and one teaspoon of anchovy sauce.

It is not apparent whether the Reverend Sydney meant an anchovy-flavoured sauce from his own kitchen, or the famous anchovy essence manufactured and bottled by Messrs Burgess, Italian and fish sauce purveyors of The Strand, London. The rhyme he uses for 'sauce' is 'toss'. Possibly he couldn't find a suitable rhyme for essence. In any case, if you can't find anchovy essence, Thai *nam pla* will do. See also Roman Relish, page 109, or maybe that's going a bit far just for a salad dressing.

In any case, who is going to spend all that money in order to try – certainly in vain – to grow six pepper plants in pots on the patio? You know what happens on patios, involving dogs, small children, cigarette ends and barbecue sauce. Life as you know it is not conducive to results like they have in the catalogue photograph, where vast quantities of shiny red and green peppery pyramids jockey for room on a wonder-bush, sunlit and windless in patio heaven.

You can read the text – *sunny border or well-placed tub* – and realise that they have accidentally omitted the words *in Acapulco*. So what will happen? Plant six seeds, four show, one nibbled by snail and dies in seed tray, plant out three, blackbird pulls one up, remaining two die from sheer misery one inclement afternoon. Either that, or they wither away into something brown and crackly because you forgot to water them on the one really hot day of the year.

Ah well, what about tomatoes? *Adapted to both glasshouse and outdoor cultivation.* Come on. We know what this means. Do not attempt to grow this variety unless you have a fully heated greenhouse, staffed twenty-four hours a day by gardeners and under-gardeners, in the warmest part of Cornwall. It will grow outdoors, but only in Cyprus.

Delicious when young. You were hoping to pick your first runner beans for tonight's supper, but they are not ready. They hang there, tiny green scimitars, their faded blossoms still attached. Next time you go, they are a foot long and not so young as they were. Hidden along the edges of each pod are strings that you must peel off with a sharp knife and which you can then use to bale hay or hang large oil paintings. After removing the strings, you are left with a substance unique in Nature, never mind unique to runner beans, a bonded, multilayered space-age total materials solution or, as we used to call it, a sandwich. This sandwich has, instead of bread, two layers of soft green rubber. Between the layers is the filling, which reminds you of the canvas used in the olden days to make tents for the army and the scouts. With only a little more maturing, this same material will be of interest to the manufacturers of Formula One racing cars.

Some words you will see in seed catalogues and elsewhere

Applied to fruit grown on perennial trees and bushes, **early** means just that. The fruit matures earlier in the season than some others. In the vegetable context, it means nothing of the sort. It does not mean that vegetable seed has to be planted early in the year, or the plants will only produce early in the season and not later, or this variety must

be planted first thing in the morning, or anything else to do with early. It simply means the variety has a shorter time to maturity than other varieties.

You can take advantage of this speed differential by planting (say) an early, a second early and a maincrop variety of potato. You plant them all at the same time, but their different times to maturity will give you new potatoes over a longer season.

If you live in cooler climes, early varieties of some vegetables are the only ones you can plant. You plant them later than does your colleague in the warmth and with any luck they'll mature before the winter starts again.

You can also use an early variety of (say) carrot for a second, late crop of small, young fingers, sown in mid summer when the carrot fly has gone, and maturing before the soil gets too cold for growth.

When selecting varieties for your allotment you will have your own priorities but, when selecting here, in this book, we have gone for tradition and flavour. There are no **F1 hybrids**, partly through the sheer pig-headedness of author and editor, and partly because many such types have been bred for commercial purposes. We have to admit to observing a slight change in this lately, as some breeders recognise that gardeners, especially allotment holders, are an expanding market for seeds and an increasingly discerning one, and their preferences do not always coincide with those of the supermarkets.

An F1 hybrid, if you didn't know, is a deliberate, hand-pollinated cross between two strains of the same vegetable, for example, two varieties of tomato, with different characteristics. They are two parents that, eventually, are going to have predictably identical offspring.

Let's say one tomato is thick-skinned, tasteless and very prolific, and one is plum shaped, juicy, delicious and resistant to blossom-end rot but an indifferent cropper.

Over a number of generations, the breeder keeps on with his two parent types, selecting and reselecting until each is exactly predictable, coming up perfectly true every time, or as near to that as is possible with a plant. He now crosses the two in-bred parents, expecting to produce a prolific, thick-skinned, tasty, plum-shaped, disease-resistant tomato with that well-known genetic characteristic, hybrid vigour.

The first generation of children are Filial One, F1. If the results are as required, they can be repeated *ad infinitum* because the parents are so true to type. Through trial and error, the breeder has found which characteristics of the two parents will emerge every time the same cross is done. And it has to be done every time with hand pollination, because F1 hybrids will not reproduce true, so there is no point in saving their seeds unless you are interested in genetics, and the parents may not be willing to mate on a commercial scale if left to themselves. The hand pollinating explains why F1s are more expensive, and why there are no F1 peas or beans (for instance), because most legumes have evolved a self-pollinating tactic and don't open their flowers to the birds and the bees.

Buying F1 seed anew each year means the breeder gets his time and money back. Fair enough, you might say, if it also means better returns for you, and sometimes it does. Certainly, it means better returns for the farmer who plants F1 hybrid seeds knowing that the result will fit in his harvesting machinery, will reach the supermarket display undamaged, and there will be lots of it on a convenient date, whatever the weather.

Most varieties of spinach offered these days in the mainstream catalogues are F1 hybrids, because the natural habits of spinach are inconvenient. One that isn't and never will be is the so-called **Perpetual** Spinach, which is neither spinach nor perpetual but a very, very good veg for your allotment. In this context 'perpetual', rather than lasting for ever without interruption, means it will bear some useful leaves through the winter and will crop again in a minor sort of way come the spring. Howsomever, having filled your freezer with the stuff and given it away by the barrowload, you may not care too much about perpetuity.

Perpetual strawberries aren't perpetual either, but do crop over a much longer period than the conventional summer type, usually with a trade-off in the flavour department.

Another word to watch is **perennial**. In certain cases, for instance rhubarb and apple, it means just exactly that. With care and attention, such perennial plants will reward you by staying alive through a number of years. Some, if you pay no attention at all, will conquer your allotment and slay every man, woman and seedling. Others, such as perennial broccoli, will attempt longevity but largely fail. Those plants that are truly perennial, such as oak trees, never have the term applied to them.

Annual means exactly that. You have to plant afresh each year because the plant completes its life-cycle in one journey around the sun or, for a cultural or climactic reason, the plant is best treated as if it did.

Hardy implies the ability to grow all through the year in the open. As is the way with implications, it often means not quite that, but only that the plant will stand through the cold weather while not necessarily growing in it. Well, that's all right, but hardy can also mean 'not really hardy if icicles hang by the wall'. Read the small print because if hardy means not necessarily being able to withstand the worst trials of a severe winter, they may be saying 'not unhardy', which is to say not half-hardy.

Half-hardy does not mean halfway to hardiness, which itself is not definable, nor imperfect hardiness, which is a characteristic displayed anyway by some allegedly hardy plants. No. Half-hardy means 'not at all hardy'. A half-hardy annual will put up with the best parts of that half of the year containing the British summer, but that's it, and that's under protest. Don't expect any more. If there's a nip in the air, your HHAs will stay nipped.

Compost is a word with two meanings. The more important is that which denotes the sweet smelling, crumbly, humuscuous delight you make from tea bags, cabbage leaves, potato peelings and other previously living material by the natural action of aerobic bacteria, which you hope will nourish your soil sufficiently if you can't get manure. The **compost bin** is that inelegantly constructed pen made out of old pallets and suchlike, containing Brussels stalks and great piles of stuff that looks like hay and dead willow herb but can't be because you didn't put any in, which refuses to turn into the aforesaid crumbly delight.

The other sort of **compost** comes in large plastic bags from the garden centre or petrol station, to be used for filling seed trays and pots. It is labelled as general purpose or as specially formulated for tomatoes, orchids, Venus fly traps and so on. Your correspondent specially formulates his by putting a quantity of crumbly delight into the wheelbarrow and mixing it with an equal quantity of garden soil put through the sieve, and a smaller amount of sharp sand if there is any.

ON MANURE

Owing to the scarcity of horses, street sweepings are now almost valueless.

Eleanor Sinclair Rohde

Compost bins need air from below and not so much from the sides, if they are to heat up and so work at a reasonable speed.

ON COMFREY

The comfrey bed should be in a sunny place where this long-lived perennial can stay undisturbed like asparagus or rhubarb. The offsets should be planted two feet apart each way in autumn or spring, and they need manure on the surface in spring (poultry droppings are ideal but any general fertiliser will do), lime in the autumn, and keeping free from weeds, especially grass. A bed holding three dozen plants ... should average 18lb each of foliage between April and November, roughly 5cwt of foliage to use and the equivalent in minerals of 1cwt of chemical potato fertiliser.

Lawrence D Hills

Mr Hills and all other authorities say comfrey seldom sets seeds, but in your humble correspondent's experience, there is no need to set off with so many plants. Just a few will self-sow all over the place. Also it will grow from the smallest bit of root, so you can easily propagate that way. Although some growers recommend comfrey as a green vegetable for the 'hungry gap', as John Seymour calls the time when the old gardening year has gone and the new has nothing yet to offer, some people may find it an acquired taste. One cwt (hundredweight) for metric folk is about fifty kilos.

Esculent, a word seen in learned and/or old descriptions of plants, is very important on the allotment because if a plant is esculent, you can eat it. *Lycopersicum esculentum* is the Latin name for tomato, the wandering peach you can eat. Another Latin word you see a lot is **sativa/us/um**, which means nothing more than 'that which is planted'. So, *Pastinaca sativa* is 'the root vegetable which is planted', *pastinaca* meaning to the Romans neither parsnip nor carrot exactly, but something in between. *Allium sativum* is the garlic which is planted, whereas *Allium capa* is the garlic which is an onion.

Forcing is a method of cheating Mother Nature by making plants believe that their time has come sooner than expected, or that they are underground and need to strive immediately to reach the sun. To make it work properly, as gardeners had to do when expected by his lordship to have pineapples and peas all year round, takes an enormous amount of skill and, usually, heating. To do it in a dilettante sort of way, for instance by putting a bucket over your rhubarb in January, will have a limited effect, possibly. Many allotment holders might think they have enough on as it is.

Ground cover in the gardening literature refers to plants that you put in deliberately, to spread widely and so strangle the weeds. In practice, ground cover plants are weeds that spread widely and strangle your French beans.

HOW TO MAKE USE OF A WEED

Infuse one ounce of dandelion in a jug with a pint of boiling water for fifteen minutes; sweeten with brown sugar or honey, and drink several teacupfuls during the day. The use of this tea is recommended as a safe remedy in all bilious afflictions; it is also an excellent remedy for persons afflicted with dropsy.

Charles Elmé Francatelli, *A Plain Cookery Book for the Working Classes*, 1851.

In the garden centre you will see kits for measuring the **pH** of your soil. Apparently, if you get a reading of 7.0 you are neutral. Less than that and you are acidic, more than that and you are alkaline. The best thing to be for veg is between 6.5 and 7.0 so, following your crop rotation scheme, you would like to be 6.5 with the occasional throwing around of some lime which, for those who didn't do chemistry at school, is your garden-friendly alkali. If you are really seriously below 6.5, you will be plagued with soil-borne pests and not have enough worms, so get that lime dug in. Plenty of muck and compost will correct over-alkalinity. Since you will be digging in compost and lime anyway, and you are far more likely to have an allotment with average-ish pH rather than one on a peat bog or a limestone pavement, acids and alkalis should not cause you sleepless nights.

A **weed** is often defined by knowledgeable folk as 'a plant in the wrong place'. The *OED* defines it as 'A herbaceous plant not valued for use or beauty, growing wild and rank, and regarded as cumbering the ground or hindering the growth of superior vegetation,' and you couldn't put it better than that. As the worshipful John Seymour says, 'Suffer not a weed to exist.'

You may be tempted to give over part of your allotment to a **wild garden**. Nothing wrong with that, except you don't normally keep stoats and rabbits next to each other. There was a fashion twenty or more years ago for wild flower gardens and your correspondent, ever keen to be up with the trends, purchased the requisite packet of mixed seeds, cut a piece of lawn very short and raked the seeds into it with vigorous endeavour. The first year it was fantastic. The second year, partly because poppies and some other flowers need annually disturbed ground, it was less so, and the third year it produced only ox-eye daisies and the noxious yellow ragwort, which now dominate motorway verges, probably for the same reason.

Chapter Three

Veg By Veg And Fruit By Fruit

So, what do we look for? Start by thinking in categories.

Permanent: fruit trees, fruit bushes, raspberries, asparagus, rhubarb;
Semi-permanent (needing occasional or gradual refurbishment or unfurbishment): strawberries, globe artichokes, most herbs, horseradish, Welsh onion, seakale, sorrel, skirret;
Seasonal/annual: everything else.

Permanent and semi-permanent plants obviously imply an area of your allotment set aside for them and them alone. Some annual/seasonal crops imply possession of a greenhouse and/or a cold frame.

Outdoor Annuals

Please note that where months are mentioned as suitable for sowing and planting, account should be taken of geographical variations implying 'sooner' or 'later'. Your correspondent, moving from Suffolk to a farmhouse 750 feet above sea level in Westmorland, was somewhat taken aback to see his broad and dwarf French beans,

---

MRS BEETON ON VEGETABLES

All vegetables should be put into boiling water, to which salt should be added in the proportion of 1 tablespoon to 2 quarts of water. The time vegetables take to boil depends on their age. Young vegetables will, as a rule, cook in about 20 minutes, whereas those fully matured will average no less than 40 minutes.

Handy to Have

A vegetable stand is ideal for kitchen use, as it saves both time and trouble. With roomy trays for holding the various vegetables required, it can be brought to the kitchen table when wanted, then stood in a cool corner to keep its contents in good condition.

Be prepared, that's the thing.

sown according to a time given by Suffolk custom and practice, gardening books and packet instructions, all cut down by successive hard frosts on the 3rd, 4th and 5th of June.

This chapter does not assume ownership of a greenhouse, although it would be nice to have one, and life without a coldframe would be difficult except in the mildest areas. We have also avoided giving detailed instructions about sowing. Once you know that the bigger the seed, the deeper it goes, common sense takes over. Similarly, there are no details on the different feeding possibilities for different plants. Being told to spread so many ounces or grams of this or that to every square foot or metre at this or that time of year only leads to confusion. If your ground is in good heart, fettled and fertile and tilled to a fine tilth (from the Anglo-Saxon verb 'tilian', to earn one's own living), your veg will grow whether you give them X quantity of potassium sulphate or not. There are a few exceptions, mentioned as we go along, the main one being the place of lime in crop rotation.

ASPARAGUS PEA, *LOTUS TETRAGONOBULUS*

Not a pea, and nothing to do with asparagus unless you convince yourself there is an asparagus hint in the flavour, this is definitely one in the 'delicious when young' category. Enjoy the cinnabar-red, sweet-pea-style flowers and pick the strange little winged pods when an inch and a half or four centimetres long at most. Beyond that they are too fibrous to eat, so better give them an inch. They want very little cooking and are excellent in a stir-fry, or lightly steamed and cold in a salad. If you miss some while picking, let them grow and hang. They'll give you many small, pea-like objects for the winter bean jar.

Cultivation follows the basic pea/bean method: soak the seeds overnight or longer, sow in seed trays, plant when they look big enough, but this is a tender, sweet little thing. Be sure frost is no longer a possibility when you put it out. Give it room to make neat, lowish bushes about two feet across, which don't need support unless you're expecting a gale.

Varieties: none.

BROAD BEAN SOUFFLÉ

You could use any vegetable for this, but beans are best, with carrots a reasonable second.

Rub some cooked broad beans through a sieve, plus a spot of cooked onion or shallot. Make an equal quantity of white sauce. For those who can't cook without measuring, you want sauce made with a quarter pint of milk and an ounce each of butter and flour, to every four ounces of bean paste, to every two lunchers.

Turn your oven on to hot, also called gas mark 6, 400°F, 200°C or thereabouts. Butter a soufflé dish, or line a deep cake tin with buttered greaseproof paper or that new stuff you can wash and re-use. Separate three eggs and beat the whites until they are as stiff as you can make them.

Stir the veg and the egg yolks into the white sauce, season with salt, pepper and mustard, or salt and Cayenne, add some finely chopped chives or another herb of choice, and gently fold in the egg whites. Turn the lot out into the cooking dish and put in the hot oven without delay. Leave it for half an hour without opening the door: this is where ovens with glass doors come into their own. Serve as soon as it's done, before it collapses.

You can hasten matters by reheating your sauce–bean mixture, but not boiling it, before taking the pan off the stove to stir in the yolks and fold in the whites. The soufflé will need much less time in the oven, maybe only ten minutes.

Tops pinched out, doing quite well, should have removed those side shoots.

BROAD BEAN, *FABA VULGARI*

One of the oldest, most widely grown, most nutritious, most prolific vegetables, the broad bean successfully sustained so many ordinary folk for so long that it became *infra dignitatem* in fashionable society. John Parkinson, royal botanist to Charles I, describes the cultivation of numerous vegetables in his book of 1629, *Paradisus Terrestris*, but dismisses broad beans as suitable for eating only by 'the poorer sort' of person.

Such is the snobbery of vegetables. This magnificent bean must be grown above all others and is one for the pest-free allotment. Enemies of the broad bean are few and easily dealt with.

The traditional way to grow them is in double rows without support, the rows a foot or so apart (an Imperial foot or your own foot), the seeds at a hand's length, the pairs of rows apart far enough to walk between.

You can sow them in the autumn, on Bonfire Night if you're an East Anglian. This should make them less liable to attack by blackfly but a really hard frost in January or February can cut them down. They'll generally come again from that setback but will crop later. Otherwise and unimpeded, they could be harvested and the plants cut off and on the compost heap in time to plant out your sprouts on the same ground – ground that has been extra-nourished with nitrogen because you have left the bean roots behind.

Although broad beans can't take persistent freezing, they are very hardy and all varieties can be sown directly into the ground in February/March, but rodents may dig them up. If you fear frost or mice, sow your beans in trays, put trays in plastic bags in the shed, give them plenty of light when they come up, ideally in a coldframe. Or, plant directly in the coldframe, and transplant. If you have the time and want to catch up a little on those autumn sowers, make newspaper tubes or cones, fill with moist potting compost and sow one bean in each. Keep upright in a box and transplant whole, including newspaper 'pot', when the greenery is two or three inches high but the roots haven't burst through yet. This avoids the shock and consequent setback of transplanting, not that it seems to bother broad beans and peas very much anyway.

The big pest is blackfly, an invasion of which is beyond the control even of several plagues of ladybirds. The fly starts off at the tops of the plants and tends to attack late-sown beans more, but is simply prevented. Pinch out the green tips of every bean plant when the first flowers, lower down, start setting to pods. By 'green tip' we mean the topmost bunch of leafy bits on the stem, removal of which prevents the plant from shooting upwards any more and demolishes the home in which aphids would otherwise squat and breed.

Not only should you thus avoid this horrible pest, but you now have handfuls of a delicious green veg. Melt a little butter or yoghurt in a pan, stir in your bean greentops for a couple of minutes and serve the moment they're hot.

If you do get blackfly, try enrobing the beasts in soapy froth from the washing-up. Otherwise, just pick the beans on each affected plant and burn the rest of it. Legend has it that summer savory sown among your beans will keep the blackfly away, and it may do. Garlic also is believed by some to be a deterrent.

Broad beans can be eaten at every stage. Juvenile pods are very good whole. The usual way is to eat the youngish fully grown seeds, also the old hard seeds in a purée, and seeds from sare pods can be kept in the winter bean jar to use as you would any other dried bean, and for planting next year.

Broad beans will take as much feeding as you can give them, so the richer the soil the better. Starting them off in a layer of wood ash is a good idea. An occasional hoeing to keep the weeds down is all the care they need, apart from pinching those tops out. You can also take out the side shoots, which are a useless distraction from the main task of podding.

Varieties: *Aquadulce*, introduced to the UK around 1850, is the usual one for autumn sowing. *Green Windsor* is probably the oldest distinct sort, pre-1800, and, if you want a prize in the produce show, you might go for another Victorian, *Masterpiece Green Longpod*. Nineteenth-century dwarf varieties such as *Land's Supreme* seem to have disappeared, superseded by *The Sutton*, 1923, the best one if you are short on space.

FRENCH BEAN (DWARF), *PHASEOLUS VULGARIS*

Also known in variety as kidney bean, haricot, flageolet, borlotti, cannelini, pinto, *et cetera*, this is another reliable, prolific and, if treated properly, pest-free plant. There are hundreds of sorts, some grown especially for the seeds, some for the pods and some for both.

Although not found in the wild, the original strains are thought by some to have been developed in South America, from that naturally occurring perennial bean of the jungle which, when privately educated, turns out as the scarlet runner. Others point to the Roman author Pliny who mentions *phaseoli*, now known as Pliny's Bean, and to Vergil who writes in his *Georgics* of *viciamque seres vilemque phaselum*, cheap vetches and beans. Scholarly opinion is that Pliny and Vergil were thinking of a fava-type, peasantish bean, that is a broad bean, rather than the more aristocratic kidney type. Either way, French beans are delicate as well as refined and so will not survive a frost.

Just as we enjoy beansprouts with our chow mein, so do slugs and snails adore the little sproutlings of the dwarf French bean. As the seeds germinate and bravely thrust their tender hooplets into the air, so down the row will come the munching gastropods to clear the lot.

As this bean has no other enemies to worry about, you may as well give it the perfect start with seed trays in a warm place rather than direct sowing. Soak the beans first, overnight. When the seedlings have two full leaves or more, and all possibility of frost is past, plant them out about six inches apart in double or triple rows also six inches apart.

Varieties: very old types were tasty but had strings, while the most modern types are totally stringless and largely taste free, such as the Kenya-air miles threadlike one you see in winter in the supermarket. Seeds of this are widely available under the name *Safari*, although why anyone would want to grow that, rather than a traditional European variety, is beyond comprehension. Some of the older but not very old varieties are claimed to be stringless and often are, but they can be 'delicious when young' if they don't happen to like the weather. *Masterpiece, Canadian Wonder, Tendergreen* and *The Prince* are very good traditional all-rounders. *Oval Yellow China* (also known as *Eureka*) and *Purple Tepee* (dwarf type) have the advantage of being clearly visible. Dwarf *Golden Butter* needs some support as it grows quite tall – but there are so many varieties you could try a different one every year and never get to the end of it.

You can pick the pods for eating whole as soon as they look big enough. Surpluses can be frozen but are better salted. Left for the season, they will all produce beans for the bean jar, but some are better than others. A good one is *Dutch Brown Bean*, but at the time of writing it seems to have gone undercover in the UK, although is widely available in Canada and, of course, Holland.

For haricots to store, when the pods are full of beans cut the plants off at the root and hang them upside down in a dry place until the pods wither. If you have a large crop it may be worth threshing them; put the pods in a cotton bag, such as the one banks used to use for coins, and whack it against something hard. Put the results through your garden sieve, winnowing as you go by tossing your beans and chaff in a strong breeze, singing your merry winnower's song. Otherwise, podding by hand saves having to fiddle about getting rid of myriad tiny flakes of old dry pod.

If you are looking specifically for beans to dry and eat through winter, climbing varieties will serve you better.

FRENCH BEAN (CLIMBING), *PHASEOLUS VULGARIS*

Cultivation is the same as for dwarf types except you have to provide the support you would give runner beans, and you get more and bigger beans. An alternative to seed trays is to build your climbing frame, set three seeds close together at the bottom of each pole and upturn a jam jar over them. When the jar is full of leaves, remove. This gives the plants a miniature greenhouse start and keeps off the slugs. You can do this also with runners.

Varieties: *Blue Lake* is the classic that everyone used to grow, a dual-purpose vegetable that gives you lots of stringless pods of excellent flavour and a good crop of haricots if you leave them to go sare. The pods of *Blue Lake* are green, not blue, whereas *Blauhilde* pods are not blue either but purple, going to green when cooked. For borlotti beans, *Firetongue* (*Lingua di Fuoco*) is the Italian classic, with red pods. A nineteenth-century yellow type, *Mont D'Or*, aka False Butter Bean, has black beans inside.

Coco blanc à rames is a classic French climbing French, also called Lazy Wife because, if you grow this bean, you have mangetout at first and later haricot so you don't need to grow any others. The name literally translates as the white chap with the oars ('chap' as in 'What ho, old bean', presumably), but more prosaically just means the tall white one.

PEA BEAN, *PHASEOLUS AEGYPTICUS*

This is a real old stager, known in Europe for centuries and nothing at all to do with peas. Grow it as you would a climbing French but keep a close eye on it when the pods are ready for picking. This is definitely one for the 'delicious when young' category as strings form very quickly once the seeds are tangible within, but no matter. Left alone, it produces a worthy crop of red–brown and white particoloured haricots for the jar.

WHEN BEANS ARE THE MEANS

The Americans were canning beans, and pork and beans, from the 1880s onwards but it wasn't until 1895 that Henry John Heinz, he of the 57 Varieties, pronounced himself satisfied with his baked beans in tomato sauce and began a long story. The recipe was sweeter back then, with brown sugar, and when Heinz's man in the UK, C H Hellen, got the beans into Fortnum and Mason he really thought he'd cracked the British market.

Alas, no, and long after the First World War there was still no sign of the Brits taking to the beans. 'I'm going to manufacture baked beans in England and they're going to like it,' said Mr Hellen and, eighty years later, a million housewives every day, plus a million a week of the Co-op's own label, plus Tesco's, plus Sainsbury's, plus HP ...

Your correspondent never has grown beans only for their seeds, preferring a dual-purpose regime, and so never has found that one type of bean provided what you might call a crop. The usual harvest goes in a couple of glass sweet jars with all the different dried beans mixed together, and very pretty they look. When the need for a beanfeast arises, a handful or several are transferred to Madame Le Creuset's pot of water, brought to the boil for ten minutes, left to soak for an hour or two, then used as below.

There is no need to soak your own beans overnight. Yours have not been machine dried. To a quantity of beans sufficient unto your needs, add more or less of:

• butter, a goodly knob, or olive oil equivalent
• an onion or two, chopped
• garlic, as much as you like
• black treacle, a good dessertspoon
• tomatoes, if you still have any preserved, or a tin of chopped if you haven't

Simmer until thick and done, on top of the stove or in a slowish oven, then add a handful of chopped fresh herbs or some you have dried, plus salt and pepper. Cayenne is good. Were you to add pork sausage and/or belly pork and/or chorizo, you would have a cassoulet.

RUNNER BEAN, *PHASEOLUS MULTIFLORUS, P.COCCINEUS*

Anyone familiar with the work of Flanders and Swann will know this, the opening of their song *Misalliance*:

The fragrant honeysuckle spirals clockwise to the sun,
And many other creepers do the same.
But some climb anti-clockwise, the bindweed does, for one,
Or Convolvulus, to give her proper name.

We cannot speculate at this distance as to the extent of Michael Flanders's botanical knowledge. Maybe he knew that runner beans are also in Nature's minority of those that climb to the left. Maybe bindweed was lyrically more suitable.

Similarities do not end there. Runner beans and the family *Convolvulaceae* are perennials with thick, fleshy roots. One of the convolvuluses produces the sweet potato in warmer climes than ours, and runners too do not like the cold, which is why we grow them as tender annuals. They like moisture also, which is why the traditional MO for the scarlet runner is the trench, dug deep as you like, filled with water-holding manure. The layer of soil on top should not reach the rim of the trench, so that vast quantities of water can more easily be guaranteed to reach their target. The water, incidentally, should not be cold from the tap. If not from your ambient water butt, it should be left to warm up first, or your flower buds may drop.

In the seventeenth century, Painted Lady was admired as an exotic flower from the jungle, and she's still going strong.

Delicious when young.

Runner beans are very prolific but, like everything else, the objective in life is to reproduce. In the case of the naturally lazy *P. multiflorus*, that means stopping all useful activity when pods reach child-bearing potential, which in turn means you have to keep picking and picking.

Some people are not keen on runner beans. They prefer the more tender texture and delicate flavour of the climbing French. Your correspondent's dear lady wife is one such, which is why we don't grow runner beans. If you happen to be the robust, peasant type – 'Fastidious folk despise this vegetable,' Eleanor Sinclair Rohde – looking for strong meat and lots of it, you cannot do better than the runner.

Various constructions can be used to support these vigorous and heavy bearing plants. True afficionados will build a mighty triangular prism (think Toblerone) from sturdy timbers, something that looks like a roof with its tiles removed. They will tie many strong strings to the ridge and will stretch them tight to the ground, fastening them with tent pegs. Up the strings and any available timbers the beans will climb and bring forth a hundred fold, or better, because the allotmenteers who do this will also have dug a deep trench, filled with well rotted manure and comfrey. Returning home in pride, they will supply the entire street with a surfeit of beans, feeding all households until they want no more.

A lesser enthusiast will make a similar sort of construction out of bamboo canes, and the level below that is the three- or five-pole tepee, still offering scope amain for a fine crop. You could put a three-pole, triangular tepee in any corner, or several corners. Plenty of liquid comfrey feed will see you sufficed.

Varieties: two of the most venerable are *Scarlet Emperor* and the red and white flowered *Painted Lady*, introduced to this country in the seventeenth century as decorative floral climbers rather than food, but still among the most popular for the kitchen and available everywhere. *Enorma* is one for the show bench, and a good old white-flowered type is *The Czar*, not so widely sold. *The Czar* is also the one for the butter bean fan, white seeded, smaller than the true butter but hardy enough for our summers, and a good cropper for the dried bean jar.

ON SALTING GREEN BEANS

Frozen runners or French beans are not much good. Well, they're all right, but salted ones are so much better. This is a job for high season when your produce is young, tender and plentiful.

Weigh about three pounds of beans. String as necessary. Slice runners and climbing French; leave dwarves whole. Mix them thoroughly with a pound of salt, then pack hard in a vessel you can get your hand into, such as a sweet jar, making sure all the salt goes in, and cover tightly. They should keep until next fresh bean season. When you want some – and this is the drawback – they need to be desalted. Soak in fresh water, rinse, soak again, rinse, taste. Steam them or boil in a very little water and tell your guests that, despite it being February 7th and snowing outside, they are fresh from the garden that day, grown by a secret method.

BEETROOT, *BETA VULGARIS*

Beetroots, like cauliflowers, are liable to react badly if checked. They want a swift, moist, uninterrupted path to usefulness, which state need not be full maturity. Beetroot, in fact, really are delicious when young. Large, oaken pickled ones, leaching their red rivers of blood across the plate, should be left in the memories of those who ate the school dinners of long ago. Better to make the borshch and lamb rogan josh unheard of in those days.

Being a root crop they will not transplant – they will bolt to seed if you try – so you must sow them where they will grow. This means your seedlings are vulnerable to slugs. Once past that danger you should have no trouble from pests, unless you are very unlucky with the beet fly on your early sowings.

Sow seeds in pairs or threes, a hand's width apart. Thin when they're big enough to go in the mixed salad and/or the pot, and pull small, young beets as they grow, leaving more room for bigger ones. If you do a latish sowing, end of May/beginning of June, you can leave your large ones to over-winter. Except in the very worst weather, they'll be all right where they are until you want them. If you predict Arctic conditions, dig a few up, screw the leaves off rather than cut, and store wrapped in newspaper. Or, cook 'em up and bottle 'em or freeze 'em.

Unchecked growth basically demands moist soil, and plenty of hoeing in dry spells. As they say in Norfolk, a good hoeing is worth a shower of rain. Sudden watering after dry weather may well shock your beets into bolting. Ideally, the soil will have been manured the previous year; fresh manure will make most root veg fork into weird shapes, offering opportunities for photo features in the local paper rather than handsome globes in the saucepan.

Varieties: *Boltardy* is the traditional one for early sowing, with its lesser inclination to

The old beetroot variety Bull's Blood gives you a visual treat in tasty salad leaves as well as fine roots.

run to seed. *Globe Crimson Globe/July Globe/Detroit Globe* is the many-named type good for big 'uns and is the one most people go for. Although not widely known until modern times, yellow beetroot have been around for 200 years. For the last fifty, the main variety has been the one introduced by that great American firm, *Burpee's Golden Globe. Bull's Blood* offers spectacularly deep red leaves for those salad thinnings. An old Italian variety, *Tonda di Chioggia*, aka *Bassano*, gives you white beet with rosy red rings. Unfortunately, as when the red T-shirt goes into the machine on hot wash with the white tennis shorts, the cooked result is a uniform pink.

SPINACH BEET, *BETA CICLA*

Also called perpetual spinach, leaf beet and embracing in colourful multiplicity Swiss chard, rhubarb chard and so on, and seakale beet (not to be confused with seakale and seakale cabbage, *q.v.*), these members of the same little family are, alongside broad beans, right at the top of the list for reliable quantity and quality, offering a massive reward for the allotmenteer in return for very little effort. They are all very good indeed, but spinach beet has the edge for hardiness and will produce greens through cold winters while the others give up. Even so, you can expect all of them to crop again, if less vigorously, when the world turns, before bolting.

The big seeds will not germinate in cold soil, so leave your sowing until spring has sprung. Start by placing seeds an inch or two apart, expecting to thin for salads and very

A mistake to make but once. You grow Swiss chard for its leaves but it's a root veg, and you don't sow root veg in seed trays and transplant.

The seedlings look all right so far and very edible, if you took a leaf or two from several, but they're going to bolt.

Thus go they to seed and wither away. Mind you, the lady planted so much it hardly matters. The freezer's full of it.

Next time, sow many fewer, where they are to stand, and they'll stay with you through winter and come again in the spring.

young cooking leaves, eventually giving your plants a good foot each way. Fresh manure in the ground doesn't matter; you don't care if the roots fork.

Slugs and snails will slide a mile for your emerging beet shoots and can annihilate your row in a night, but protection against these, the only real enemy, will assure you of sackloads of spinach. Confronted by a packet of seeds with hundreds in, most people will sow too many and end up putting barrowloads on the compost heap. In any case, pick the big old leaves for composting, to encourage more young ones.

Cooking instructions generally suggest using the mature stems and leaves separately, and this is not a bad idea if the leaves are very large. Young whole leaves need the merest kiss of steam, or wilting with a knob of butter. What looks a lot makes but a little, but excellent.

THEY HAVE ONLY THREE VEGETABLES

... and two of them are cabbage.

Walter H Page, US Ambassador
to the Court of St James, 1913–1918.

Varieties: an old one called *Rainbow* gives you multi-coloured chard. *Swiss Chard* is red stalked, usually, but the name is also given sometimes to *Silver* or *Seakale Beet/Chard*, which is white stalked like the stalwart head of the family, the simple perpetual spinach.

BRASSICA

Broccoli, Brussels sprouts, cabbage, cauli, kale, couve tronchuda, kohl rabi, most of the brassica family, follow the same basic methods of cultivation, fit in the same place in your crop rotation, have the same enemies and vary only in their time of year, so it makes sense to treat them together. Turnips and swedes, although of the family, are root veg so follow a non-transplanting system and are treated separately.

For the rest, sow in a seed tray or well-limed seed bed; transplant when the seedlings have three or four proper leaves. If you have plenty of room, one transplanting will do. If you need to wait for new potatoes, early peas or something else to come out, moving your brassicae to a nursery bed and keeping them going there will do them no harm at all. Give these adolescents four or five inches either way.

In fact, the second transplanting to their final positions may well give better results because the roots tend to proliferate. In any case, they like firm ground to grow in. Tread well and hard, and doubly hard for your sprouts.

The main enemies are club root, root fly and caterpillars, closely followed by flea beetles, the larvae of various moths, wireworms, *et cetera, et cetera*. Sometimes it seems that every living creature wants a meal off your brassica plants and if, through sound practice with your soil and your crop rotation, and proper use of safe and traditional remedies, you manage to rear a whole range of gorgeous greens, along come the wood pigeons one early winter's morning and skin your sprouting broccoli.

One extra thing to do with brassicae, or rather not to do, is never leave your sprout and cabbage stumps in the ground for so-called 'spring greens'. What you get isn't worth the increased hospitality you are thus giving to enemies.

All of these plants, in their infinite variety and usefulness, have been bred over many, many centuries from the species and sub-species of a wild plant, *Brassica oleracea*, often called sea cabbage because it likes the seaside. Like common sense, it is not as common as it used to be, but prehistoric man would have found it plentiful if almost too bitter to eat until he discovered boiling and then, perhaps, changing the water and boiling again.

BORECOLE, *BRASSICA OLERACEA ACEPHELA*

More widely known as kale, this family of the cabbage tribe is largely resistant to the pests and diseases affecting the rest, grows under almost any circumstances and is the hardiest of the lot. This may go part way to explaining why it is the peasants' cabbage (from the Dutch *boer*, a peasant or farmer, *kool*, a cabbage), it being so brutally unrefined as to survive in all extremities. Also, it has been around since the year dot and so cannot be fashionable or interesting to those in the vanguard of society.

Another factor may be the flavour of some kales, particularly when mature, which is too strong for delicate palates. Howsomever, peasants can't be choosers. Peasants want to pick fresh kale for dinner whatever the weather, while everyone else must resort to freezer or greengrocer.

Varieties: various kinds of *Curled*, including *Dwarf Green, Tall, Half Tall* and *Up*, also the *Thousand Headed*, are the ones most people recognise. *Asparagus Kale* is a flat-leafed sort; *Cavalo Nero* has dark blue-green, long leaves something like a slim-line Savoy crossed with a primrose. *Ragged Jack* has frilly purplish leaves as if a red cabbage has mated with a dandelion and gone mad; *Chou de Russie* or *Red Russian* is very similar to *Ragged Jack* and some seed merchants sell it as the same thing.

A talking point for the allotment would be the *Jersey Tree* or *Walking Stick*, called cabbage but actually a kale. It grows taller than you, sometimes much taller, and is largely used as cattle fodder – but then some would say this is the true purpose of all kales. *Scotch Kale* is either the general name for the curled types, or a name for a blueish, dwarfish variety that looks exactly similar to *Thousand Headed*, or it's a staple dish of Scotland (see recipe).

Variegated Kale, generally sold in the flower seeds section as Ornamental Kale, is as edible as any other but comes in dozens of colours, shapes and sizes. Plant three or four Jersey Trees with ornamentals scattered at their feet and take a photograph for the pub quiz.

Flanders Purple Borecole, or Flanders Kale
(1/12 natural size).

SCOTCH KALE

Recipe published in 1896:

> Put barley on the fire in cold water, and when it boils take off the scum; put in any piece of fresh beef and a little salt; let it boil three hours; have ready a colander full of kale, cut small, and boil it tender. Two or three leeks may be added with the greens if the flavour is approved of. This broth is also made with salted beef; which must be put in water overnight to soak.

By this the author, George Augustus Sala, *Daily Telegraph* leader writer, war correspondent, artist, collector and spendthrift, meant to make a soup derived from the original dish, which, according to Mrs Beeton, 'is the *Pot-au-feu* of Scotland, and, like its Continental prototype, may have the meat served separately or in the broth'. Mrs B recommends a piece of mutton of about one and a half pounds rather than beef, and onions as well as leeks, to be cooked in two quarts of water for three hours, plus another hour with the kale added. You take out the meat at the end, cut it up, put the pieces in a tureen, pour over the broth and serve. Sufficient for four or five persons.

SPROUTING BROCCOLI, *B. OLERACEA BOTRYTIS APARAGOIDES/CYMOSA*

Leaving aside those styles of broccoli that are indistinguishable from cauliflowers, and treating calabrese as a separate item, we are left with the purple and the white sprouting. These are magnificent vegetables, generally recovering from anything the cabbage white butterfly can do and producing one of the most palatable forms of green vegetable food at a time when it is especially welcome. Unless you are prey to wood pigeon attack, you can usually rely on good old sprouting broccoli to deliver lots of good stuff over a lengthy, wintry period.

They are big plants, so give them two or three feet each way, and harvest some sproutings from each rather than stripping one entirely. Seed sown in late spring should give you broccoli well into the hungry gap.

Varieties: new commercial strains produce in the autumn and you can see a mild-flavoured, non-floppy version of purple sprouting in the shops for half the year, when before you hardly saw it at all. Real sprouting broccoli in the proper season remains a matter for the old varieties. *Early* or just plain *Purple* and *White Sprouting* are equally good and both were well known in the eighteenth century. The white is supposedly less hardy although your correspondent has not noticed any difference.

Nine Star Perennial is an introduction from the 1930s that makes a goodly number of small, white, cauli-type heads and, left to stand and pruned a bit, is claimed to do the same next year and for years thereafter. Personal experience suggests that annually diminishing returns make this large plant not worth its space unless you have excess of same and can't be bothered with the more bountiful annual kinds.

BRUSSELS SPROUTS, *B. O. BULLATA GEMMIFERA*

The shape of the classic Brussels plant reminds you of an Edwardian lady in a big hat. There is curvature to it, a swelling plenty of large and small, that has been entirely lost in the F1 hybrids that now dominate the seed catalogues. These new types produce vast quantities of hard, fast, regimental buttons of very similar size all along a straight trunk in perfect spiral order, which is exactly what the supermarkets want. Fine. OK. No problem. Grow a knobbly telegraph pole if you want. If you'd rather grow an Edwardian lady in a big hat, read on.

Regarding that big hat – the displays in recent years of sprout tops in greengrocers' shops are due to the equally recent, widespread capability of buying sprouts, F1 hybrids of course, by the whole stem. F1 hybrid sprouts tend to readiness all at once along said stem, whereas old varieties produce gradually from the bottom up. Removal of the plant top halts production and makes the sprouts already produced fluff out (blow), so these hat-style delicacies on traditional sprouts should not be gathered until that plant has done all its work, by which time you might not fancy them.

One allotment neighbour will tell you never to cut your sprouts but always to snap them off. Another will tell you the opposite. Whichever advice you follow, take your

buttons a few at a time and, as with sprouting broccoli, don't strip a plant entirely until the very end. Gardening lore also says sprouts need frost to develop their full flavour; it ain't necessarily so, but could well be. Certainly, the red types seem to have better colour and flavour after frost and if you have trouble with grey aphids on your buttons, the frost sees them off too.

Varieties: some seed catalogues offer nothing but F1 hybrids. From the early part of the twentieth century, *Bedford Fillbasket* is still around, and *Evesham Special* can be obtained with difficulty. Other traditional varieties such as *Dwarf Gem* and *Darlington* seem to have disappeared but *Noisette* (small and very tasty), *Roodnerf Early Button* (resistant to blowing) and the late variety *Cambridge No 5* are still to be found if you look hard enough. Your correspondent's favourite for taste is the big, late, red one, *Rubine*, a delight for the table although no prizewinner for quantity. Another good red one is *Falstaff*.

Whichever you grow, we re-emphasise the importance of firm ground and ask you to keep that hoe going. One weed in particular, the extremely common shepherd's purse, harbours pests of Brussels and other brassicae. You'll know it even if not by name. It looks kind of dandelionish in the leaf and throws up long thin spikes of tiny white flowers, which turn into little heart-shaped seed pods – but you won't let it get that far, will you.

BROCCOLI CALABRESE, *B. O. ITALIC*

When George Bush Senior became President of the USA and expressed his joy that nobody now could make him eat broccoli, it was calabrese he was talking about, the broccoli of Calabria, rare in the UK until fairly recently. Its chief difference from our traditional sprouting broccoli, and its chief benefit, is its short time to maturity, making it an autumn treat. However, it is not hardy. Frost may kill its lurking caterpillars but it kills the vegetable too.

The plants are smaller than purple and white sprouting, producing a central, cauli-type head – the one you see in the shops – and, after you've taken that with a knife, small subsidiary heads around.

Varieties: the older strains are Italian, of course, and the only one you'll find in mainstream catalogues is the one we saw first in the UK, usually called *Green, Green Heading* or *Autumn Calabrese*. Most of the rest on offer are tasteless F1 hybrids and other types developed for the commercial market but it is easy to find one of the very best old strains, *De Cicco*, which produces only a smallish central head but lots of side shoots and, flavour wise, is the reason why the Italians like broccoli so much.

CABBAGE, *B. O. CAPITATA*

It is perfectly possible to pick a cabbage from your allotment every day of the year, if you like cabbage that much, and the various strains can be divided by the seasons: spring, summer, autumn, winter, and red.

The basic routine is to sow in the autumn for spring greens, sow in the spring for fast-growing summer cabbages and slower autumn ones, and in the summer for the hardy types that will mature and stand obdurately through the dark days of winter. Planting out is done on well-firmed ground that has been limed, thus. Take a small handful of slaked lime, or 4 ounces, or 113.5 grams, and scatter it over a square yard, or a square metre. Repeat as necessary. Hoe or rake it in, then stamp along your row, making holes with a dibber. The smaller spring and summer cabbages need a foot each way, bigger ones a foot and a half.

Let us begin in July, or August if you live in a frost-free zone. Sow your spring cabbage seeds in tray or bed, ready for planting out in early autumn, ideally where your potatoes were. If you sow in a seed bed, cover the seeds not with soil but with a sifted mixture of wood ash and lime. This should help prevent enemies from attacking. You can also sow under glass for earlier planting, if you're hoping for a prize at the produce show or if you're a cabbage-a-day person.

In March sow quick-growing types to plant in April for summer use and slower ones for autumn use, including reds, or sow the quickies again in May. Also in May sow your big beasts for the winter, also including reds if you want them to stand until spring comes again.

Varieties: cabbage has a very long history and there are dozens of traditional varieties still about. For spring greens into the hungry gap, the great old favourite is *Offenham 2 Flower of Spring*, and another good one is *Wheeler's Imperial*, both widely available. Harder to find is *Ellam's Early*, less liable to bolt in a mild springtime. Fast-growing strains for spring sowing and summer eating include pointy-headed *Greyhound* and a more recent addition (1929), ball-headed *Golden Acre Primo*. *Winningstadt* is a nineteenth-century, slower growing, pointy cabbage, which should last you well into the autumn. *Brunswick* is an even older ball-headed equivalent that can grow very large indeed. *Red Drumhead* is an eighteenth-century type that is good for pickling and even better for casseroling with robber pigeons, should you manage to take any into custody.

For the winter, *January King* is very hard to beat, and the Savoy type *Ormskirk*, and *Christmas Drumhead*, although the latter is not so late standing.

CAULIFLOWER, *B. O. BOTRYTIS CAULIFLORA*

The flowered cabbage, 'the young inflorescence of which forms an edible head' (*Shorter Oxford Dictionary*), is a vegetable greatly abused by commerce. So anxious have supermarkets and their suppliers been to offer perfectly white, perfectly rounded caulis, with florets so tightly packed no caterpillar could possibly get in, that the merest hint of flavour has been lost.

Don't worry, little fellow. You'll be the size of a beachball next week.

Cauliflower always was regarded as a delicate and aristocratic vegetable, at the opposite end of the brassica social scale to borecole, and early methods of cooking can't have helped preserve the taste. In 1822 they were boiling caulis whole in a cloth.

Caulis are also tender fellows in the weather, but different growing regimes can offer produce over a long season. The simplest is to sow in trays in March/April and plant out once all danger of frost is past. Earlier sowings in the warm will bring your cutting season forward. Keeping some of the later-sown plants in a nursery bed while new spuds and peas finish can give you caulis in November. Autumn sowings under glass should give you young plants for setting out in March, if you can then protect them. Follow the treading/liming planting procedure as for cabbages and all the rest of the family.

Caulis do not like hot dry spells or any other check on their smoothly rapid growth, so keep them well watered and hoed. They also have a terminal dislike of frost, or at least the inflorescence does, but Jack can be kept at bay, for a short while anyway, by folding big outside leaves over the flowered head.

Varieties: *Snowball* and *Veitch's Autumn Giant* (aka *Giant of Naples*) are nineteenth-century types universally applauded. *All The Year Round* is from the 1930s and very popular. *Walcheren Winter 5* may stand checks and cold weather better than some. *Sicilian Violet* may look like a gimmick but it has been around since mid Victorian times.

All of these varieties promise you much better flavour than their commercial cousins but they are susceptible to inconvenient weather, they do need looking after, and each sowing is liable to turn in all at once. The kitchen can get over-cauliflowered. While everyone knows about cauli in white sauce, cheese sauce, tomato sauce, soup and fritters, and My Lady Delia's recipe for cauli with garlic and bacon is well worth making, especially if you add some ground hazelnuts. You may not have tried making a dessert from it ...

GOBI KHEER

Cut the flowery bits very fine from one or more cauliflowers, until you have about a pound of granular material. Put it and six cardamoms into four pints of whole milk and cook gently until thick. Add eight ounces white sugar, plus two ounces each of ground almonds, desiccated coconut, raisins and chopped hazelnuts, and a few drops of rosewater or almond essence. Cook until the consistency is as desired. Pour into a classy bowl and sprinkle with a little cinnamon and a few rose petals. Quite unauthentically, this is very nice served with amaretto biscuits.

CHOOSE CAULIFLOWERS

... that are close and white, trim off the decayed outside leaves, and cut the stalk off flat at the bottom. Open the flower a little in places to remove the insects, which generally are to be found about the stalk, and let the cauliflowers lie in salt and water for about an hour previous to dressing them, with their heads downwards; this will effectually draw out all insects. Put them* into fast-boiling water, with the addition of salt in the above proportion, and let them boil gently, keeping the saucepan uncovered. The water should be well-skimmed.

(*Presumably Mrs B, for it is she, means the caulis, not the insects)

COUVE TRONCHUDA, *B. O. COSTATA*

Also called seakale cabbage and Portuguese cabbage, this is a big plant making a double offering, the ribs and the leafy bits, to cook separately. It is a very hardy, non-heading cabbage like the spring greens in the shops and, while winning no prizes for delicacy of flavour, it can be there when all else has deserted. The only cultural difference to other brassicae is the room it needs for full development: three feet each way.

KOHL RABI, *B. O. CAULORAPA*

Sometimes thought to be a Victorian import from Germany – the name is German, translating approximately as 'cabbage turnip', and the Victorians loved it – kohl rabi is mentioned in much earlier English texts. It may well have been bred in Germany, certainly northern Europe, around 1500 and from there found its way to many parts. It's basically a cabbage/Brussels/broccoli stalk distended and rendered more palatable.

It rather fell out of favour in the twentieth century, becoming a curiosity to most people, who preferred turnips anyway, but, not being root crop, kohl rabi can be a useful alternative in some allotments. The temptation always is to let it stand too long, watching those sputniks swell, but when they get big and old they're useful only for playing handicap croquet. If the plants are checked earlier by a hot, dry spell you can also end up with wooden golf balls.

Assuming uninterrupted progress, most cooks of the old school will tell you to pick them when tennis/cricket ball size and boil them whole, skins on. Instead, you might like to peel them, chip them and give them a rapid steaming or stir-frying. If the latter, add a dollop of oyster sauce.

Varieties: *Purple Vienna* and *White Vienna* are the two main traditional ones. *Purple Vienna* is white on the inside, *White Vienna* likewise but green on the outside. Modern types are said to be less prone to mahogany syndrome, but don't bank on it.

CARDOON, *CYNARA CARDUNCULUS*

This delicately flavoured veg was ever popular with those who ate at great tables and so didn't have to produce it in the garden. Its drawbacks include a long growing season yet tenderness to cold weather, large appetite, large size, and it needs blanching. The old way of dealing with it is in a trench, like celery, so it's easier to feed, water and earth up, but the trench needs to be First World War size.

It's also a tremendous faff to prepare and cook, and it's very invasive, considered a serious nuisance weed in some countries. Just as we look at the pink, white and green of Himalayan balsam blocking our previously babbling brooks and wonder what it is (it's Himalayan balsam), so do Argentineans and Australians look at cardoons. If you were to grow cardoon and let it go to seed, it being spectacular like a gigantic thistle crossed with a palm tree, you could find yourself up before your local Torquemada and the Allotment Inquisition.

Varieties: none but the *Common Cardoon.*

CARROT, *DAUCUS CAROTUS*

Wild carrots like sandy soil and so do your tame ones. One gardening ancient reported the test for good carrot ground as being the ability to thrust in a walking stick up to the handle, but he was probably thinking about the show bench. Certainly, success comes more easily with lighter soils, so if you're on heavy clay, the more compost, wood ash, leaf mould, sharp sand and so on you can dig in, the better.

If you feel confident about beating the carrot fly, sow when you like after the end of March when the soil has warmed up a little. Otherwise sow in February/March under cloches or leave it until mid May/June using the quick-growing types and you will avoid the worst of the fly, because you won't be thinning when she's about. Sow very thinly and aim to make your first thinning for bite-size saladings. If a second thinning looks necessary, resolve to sow with more care next time.

Varieties: many of the old sorts were bred for maincrop cultivation and winter storage, so size and keeping qualities were important. Very few modern allotmenteers are going to bother with burying carrots in sand, and so can look more for flavour and exuberance by picking while younger and smaller in summer and autumn. The list of the best old strains is music to the ears of silvery-whiskered old gardeners such as your correspondent: *Amsterdam Forcing, Early Nantes, James's Scarlet Intermediate, Chantenay Red Cored, Autumn King* – all nineteenth- or early twentieth-century developments and all widely available today.

Amsterdam Forcing is quick growing and ideal for a June sowing, likewise *Early Nantes*. *James's Intermediate* can grow long and deep and so prefers the lighter soils but will grow almost anywhere in any weather. *Chantenay* too can grow large and was widely used commercially for maincrop before uniformity was the thing; some supermarkets sell it now as a gourmet carrot. *Autumn King* will produce its cylindrical roots where the soil is not carrot-perfect but is said to be especially alluring to the fly.

The aforementioned silvery-whiskered one will plump for *Early Nantes* for taste, closely followed by *Amsterdam Forcing*, but they're all good. As a friend of his once exclaimed while eating some as crudités: 'Hey! These are real carrots!'

CELERIAC, *APIUM GRAVEOLENS RAPACEUM*

Turnip-rooted celery may seem to many readers a parvenu but it was popular in Victorian and earlier gardens because of its long eating season and good storage qualities. The shoots and leaves (delicious when young) above the turnip can be used as celery but test first for bitterness. Like kohl rabi, the fat bit, the swollen stem, requires a dampish growing time without dry-spell interruption.

However, it is a long growing time, starting with germination in warmth (seed tray, carrier bag, airing cupboard) in February/March, and that can take three or four weeks. Prick out at some stage and keep under glass. Plant out when frost is a memory and the plants look big enough – could be ten weeks or more from sowing – giving a foot each way, trying not to submerge the beginnings of their swelling balls. This is a form of celery so has a hearty appetite and will take as much liquid manure as you care to give it.

Younger, smaller balls are good for salads or brief cooking; the pure-white flesh will discolour on peeling unless you give it a swift lemony dressing or, if you are going to cook it, a bath in acidic water. Better, slice it into apple or orange juice, bring to the boil therein and simmer until tender.

In milder regions, big old balls can be left where they stand. Where winters bite hard, they may be worth protecting with some straw thrown over, or dig them up and store where they won't dehydrate.

Varieties: few of the older ones are still easily available. *Prague Giant*, aka *Large Smooth Prague*, is one, a nineteenth-century strain said to have been developed from *Erfurt*, which also can still be found. The celeriac you see in the shops is likely to be *Monarch*, a slightly more beautiful, commercial enlargement of the *Prague Giant* type.

CELERY, *APIUM GRAVEOLENS*

Wild celery, common in areas that are both damp and near the sea, has the same Latin name as the cultivated sort, and the same taste only more so. Its powerful smell, something like a whole family of celery-type veg rotting down in hot weather, does put people off but the leaves when dried make a perfect celery-flavour additive, and the stems aren't bad, in moderation.

Cultivated celery has much fatter, crisper stems, no strong smell and is an all-round milder being. That green 'celery' you see palely loitering in the supermarket is so innocuous that only the crispy texture remains, enraging the celery enthusiast who proclaims the true, flavourful virtues of proper celery in winter and is, moreover, willing to undertake all that trench carry-on to get it.

Proper celery needs blanching and, if you are going to dream of thick winter stews, shin of beef casserole, mutton hotpot, with large chunks of lovely celery discernable within, you need to follow one of two regimes: trench, or earthworks.

The basic routine is the same for both. Sow seed as for celeriac, grow on in the richest soil possible, with neat manure incorporated if need be, and keep moist. When summer is nearly done and the plants are well towards mature size, the stems must be blanched, that is, turned pale and tender by sealing them off from the light. If they are to stand into the winter, the blanching must also protect from frost.

Whether you choose to do all this by putting the plants in a trench and earthing them up by gradually filling in the trench, or by building a kind of long ziggurat of soil along the row with your plants inside, a living pie as it were, is up to you. Both are equally hard work and require just as much attention.

Before earthing up, the stalks of the plants need to be drawn together. The usual way is to tie them with string and put a paper collar around to stop soil working its way inside the bunch, not only to avoid grit in your teeth later but to prevent micro- and other organisms in the soil defeating you by creeping in and initiating brown unpleasantness from the inside.

It's good to have a pal with you when you start this earthing process. One of you holds the leaves while the other ties the string. Lawrence D Hills, who favoured the above-ground ziggurat technology, suggested a solo method using your garden line. Peg in at the start of the row, hold the leaves of the first plant while you wind a loop around, run the string on to the next, wind around, and so on. Peg in at the other end. Go back, break off any side shoots at the base of each plant, and earth up, initially to about three inches. Retrieve string. This would be around the middle of August, if your plants are in time with Mr Hills's. Do it again about three weeks later, and again, by which time you'll be earthing right up to the leaves. Pat your pie firm with a spade or a cricket bat.

The whole point of all this palaver is to have celery in the depths of winter, so you may think that soil alone is insufficient protection. Having gone to ziggurat-building trouble, you may as well belt-and-brace it by adding paper collars at the first earthing or, even better, something more insulating, long-lasting and grit-preventing. Very heavy-duty paper such as they make feed sacks from, or corrugated cardboard, would be good, or ordinary jute sacking.

The pest you are most likely to encounter, apart from slugs, earthworms and other small things burrowing into badly earthed up stems, is the celery fly. The larvae excavate a channel between the membranes of the leaves, leaving intricate brown paths, which, if unattended, will join together to destroy the leaf entirely, depriving the plant of vital function. Pick off leaves with mines in, and spray with nicotine and soft soap mixture (see page 142).

Varieties: *Giant Red*, *Golden Self Blanching* and *Giant Pascal* are all nineteenth-century varieties. 'Self blanching' then meant 'a little blanching will be enough'. *Hopkins Fenlander* is another good old one. Modern varieties that are as they are without blanching, for example of the flavourly-challenged *American Green* type, are not hardy enough for winter use.

CHERVIL, *CHÆROPHYLLUM BULBOSUM*

Like small, short carrots to look at, this is a vegetable long popular on mainland Europe where they seem more willing to put in a little extra work if there are gourmet consequences. It's been in Britain certainly since the mid eighteenth century but has made little impact, so little indeed that it is not even mentioned in many of the august and heavy publications purporting to be 'encyclopædias' of gardening. Howsomever, you can still get the seeds, sometimes under the name of turnip-rooted chervil, parsnip-rooted chervil, or just plain root chervil. It is not at all the same thing as the herb chervil, one of the French *fines herbes*, which looks rather like sweet cicely, and it doesn't really taste quite like any other vegetable.

'Tis a full year a-growing and the seeds will not keep, so use them all. Sow in September, under cloches in the colder regions, and thin out to an inch or two apart. The little roots will be ready when the foliage dies back next September, but better to leave them to get a touch of frost. Wash them well but don't peel. Steam them whole and serve likewise, or put them in a casserole or soup.

CHICORY, *CICHORIUM INTYBUS*

Less of a challenge than celery are the three blanching winter salads, chicory, its relative endive and seakale, all of which can also be cooked. Sow chicory April/May *in situ* and watch out for slugs, or in a seed tray. Thin/plant out about a foot each way or less. Pests don't seem to bother from then on, so it's routine maintenance only until a few weeks before you might need some for the table.

The odd thing about it is that the plant you can see is not the plant you want. Dig her up carefully with a fork and cut off all her leaves, leaving only short stubble on the crown. Put the root in the corner of a box that has some damp potting compost, fine soil, moley borings or similar in the bottom and, if it's plastic, drainage holes. Repeat, putting roots side by side until you can't cram any more into your box. Fill all spaces between with compost or whatever you've used, leaving only the stubble showing. Cover the box with something that will allow air but not light.

If the place of blanching is at ambient winter temperature, you can expect to find crisp, white leaves in four or five weeks, sooner if the place is a bit warmer. The same roots will give you another cropping. To extend your season into the hungry gap, leave more roots in the ground for later digging.

Varieties: *Witloof* is universal. *Barbe de Capucin* is the French, looser-topped one if you can get it.

CUCUMBER, *CUCUMIS SATIVUS*

This fruit is mainly dealt with under greenhouse varieties. Even more than tomatoes it requires a good summer to succeed as an outdoor crop. The method is the same as for marrows and courgettes, to which it is closely related, giving it a little hill or ridge to sit on and ramble over when by nature it would rather be climbing. Dig a hole for the base of each hill to hold a thick layer of moisture-retaining stuff – manure, leaves, half-rotted compost, newspapers – with a good foot or more of soil above and giving each plant a square yard of space. The seeds need a comfortable start, in a nice, warm place,

Three different chicories in youthful vigour: to the left, red stalked Italian dandelion; at the front, rossa di Treviso; on the right, Witloof.

so sow them in pairs in small pots, cover with plastic bags and put them in the airing cupboard. Do this in April, and transplant to larger pots. Harden off the plants in a coldframe or make other arrangements to keep them growing without exposure to cool days and cold nights, and aim to plant out at the end of May.

If June doesn't look like being all that flaming, cloches or a clear polythene tent might compensate but make sure the pollinating insects can get in. If July and August are cold and wet, you will have wasted your time. What outdoor cucumbers really object to, as indeed do their indoor brethren, is rapid and large changes of temperature. You can control this to an extent in a glasshouse. Outdoors you are at the mercy of Michael Fish.

Cucumbers grow on side shoots. Pinch out the top of the main stem when you can see half a dozen sets of leaves. In theory you should also pinch out the side shoots to allow one fruit per shoot but, in a good season, you'll have a job doing that with some of them.

Varieties: many of the ridge types were meant for pickling. *White Wonder* is an old Italian strain which does for pickles when small and salads when larger and is quite easy to find, likewise *Cornichon de Paris* which, in the aforesaid good summer, gives you squillions of one-inch picklers. *Long Prickly* goes back to the eighteenth century and, like other old boys, can have a rather bitter skin.

CUT A CUCUMBER

... in our Garden this morning that measured in length eleven Inches and a half.

The Diary of a Country Parson, James Woodforde, August 10th, 1794.

ENDIVE, *CICHORIUM ENDIVIA*

With chicory and seakale, endive makes up the trio of blanching winter delicacies. Endive has two basic types: the curly, which looks like ornamental kale that's had an Afro, and the not quite so curly Scarola or Batavian type, more useful for cooking. Batavia is not an obscure, vegetable-growing republic of central Europe but the old capital of the Dutch East Indies, on the coast of Java.

Sowings can be made right through the season, from March in milder parts and on to September. Most allotmenteers will make a sowing in April for summer use and a change from lettuce, and in July for the winter. The blanching methods are as for chicory.

Varieties: the main curly one, called *frisée* in French, is *Moss Curled*. The very hardy and sometimes rather bitter Batavian can be had as *Winter of Bordeaux*.

FENNEL, *FŒNICULUM DULCE* or *FŒNICULUM VULGARE AZORICUM*

In its native Italy called finocchio and otherwise Florence or Florentine fennel, its aniseedy bulbs are found delicious by those who like aniseed. It need not be much trouble to grow although it does need plenty of water and, because it's really a perennial grown as an annual, spring sowings run a risk of bolting, especially if there's a cold spell or any check in growth. As with any tenderish plant there are various options for cultivation. Sow early under glass or sow in mid spring where it is to stand and plant or thin to nine inches each way. In mild areas, another sowing in the summer will bring in an autumn crop. A more rapid regime assumes a greenhouse: sow in pots in May, keep warm, plant out in early July, harvest in August.

Whichever way you go, it's a greedy feeder. Some authorities recommend earthing up the swelling bulbs. Be prompt with your harvesting; as soon as the bulb is, in the plant's opinion, fully mature, it's time to send up a flower stalk and that will wither the bulb.

Varieties: one from the seventeenth century is *Sweet Florence*.

Florence fennel, grown mainly for its aniseedy bulb, is not to be confused with bronze fennel, Fœniculum vulgare purpureum, a leaf-only herb that seeds itself everywhere.

GARLIC, *ALLIUM SATIVUM*

There's not much to growing garlic. Stick the cloves in the ground in February and dig up when the leaves die. Don't leave it any longer or the withered bit of leaf will be gone and you won't be able to find your crop beneath the weeds. Ripen the bulbs on a sack in the sun before hanging up to store. Larger bulbs will come from autumn planting but you will have to protect them from frost, for instance with a straw mulch, especially the softneck types.

You may like to grow rather more garlic than you can eat, so you can use it for pest control (see page 141). If so, do not use any artificial fertilisers as this seems to reduce the garlic's potency as an insecticide.

Varieties: there are hundreds nowadays, mainly dividing into softnecks and hardnecks. The hardnecks are potentially more trouble because they send up a stalk, called a scape, which 'flowers' into a head with little bulblets or bulbils, taking energy from where you want it. Seeking large bulbs, the purist will cut off the heads as they form. Or, you can leave them and plant the bulbils to make garlic-flavoured salad greens or, if you leave them again, single cloves. Hardneck bulbs have a stronger flavour generally, and are hardier in the ground, but they don't store so well. Possibly the best-known old variety is *German Red*.

Softnecks store very well, right around the year if kept cool, and these are the ones for making plaits. *Solent Wight* is a well-tried one. On the other hand, rather than chasing expensive seedsman's stock, you could buy some nice-looking bulbs much more cheaply from the farmers' market and follow the detailed cultural instructions above.

The wild Sand Leek, *A. scorodoprasum*, a close relative of garlic, is sometimes called Rocambole from the Scandinavian words for 'onion of the rocks' and sometimes cultivated. It has a mild, garlicky flavour. The Rocambole hardneck garlics, which are popular in America and widely cultivated there, are nothing to do with it.

HAMBURG PARSLEY, *PETROSELINUM CRISPUM TUBEROSUM*

In effect half parsley, half parsnip, it does for both but isn't quite as good as either. The leaves you can cut and use as you would parsley and the roots look like inferior parsnips but don't taste quite the same. Still, they are hardy and can be left until wanted. Like all members of its family, it is slow to germinate.

Varieties: none.

JERUSALEM ARTICHOKE, *HELIANTHUS TUBEROSUS*

'Girasol' is a sixteenth-century English word for sunflower, derived from the same French and Spanish word and the Italian *girasole*, and *H. Tuberosus* will indeed produce big yellow flowers in climes slightly warmer than ours. The nationality is not known of the explorer who found the native Americans growing and eating this plant, and who thought it tasted a little like the artichokes back home. Eventually it found its way to the London markets, where the cheery traders mispronounced girasol as Jerusalem and so that's what we call a vegetable that is nothing like an artichoke.

An equally interesting explanation of the name is that the Dutch settlers of New Amsterdam cultivated this same American plant and shipped it back to Terneuzen, in Holland, whence it arrived in London markets in 1622. The cheery traders couldn't say 'Terneuzen' either, so it became the more familiar Jerusalem, and this must be the true version because the word 'girasol' wasn't current then. Ah, but it was, first recorded in writing in 1586, so the girasols have it.

There are various ways of propagating. The easiest is to go in wintry season down to the greengrocer's and pick out a pound of his biggest and best-looking tubers. Stick them in the ground about two feet apart each way, a good six inches deep, and you'll never get rid of them. The more room they have and the richer the soil, the less likely you are to curse them for being knobbly, twisted and difficult to deal with in the kitchen. They like lime too.

They will grow six or seven feet tall and frost will denature the stems, so cut these off, leaving a locating stub. The tubers can stay where they are until you want to dig some. They tend to make a kind of thick interwoven wheel that you should try to get up whole. Your inevitable failure to do so will result in more growth next year whether you want it or no.

The legend says that anyone entertaining HM Queen Elizabeth II is forbidden from serving JA soup because of its flatulence-causing properties. True or not, HM Queen Delia does not mention any such matter in her recipe for carrot and artichoke soup, which is simply made with common-sense quantities of JAs, carrots, celery, onion, butter and vegetable stock, with crème fraîche and parsley to garnish. Isabel James of the McCarrison Society for Nutrition and Health follows similar lines but without the carrots, and with milk instead of stock and oil instead of butter. JAs can also substitute for water chestnuts in salads and Chinese recipes, and they go well in a mixed pickle.

Varieties: not a great deal of effort seems to have gone into breeding different strains. Greengrocer's or *Common* is one. *Fuseau* is another, allegedly less knobbly.

LAND CRESS, *BARBAREA PRÆCOX/VERNA*

You can look at your allotment in winter and not see very much green stuff, except in that damp corner where you had the foresight to sow some land cress, aka American cress although it's a European native. As its name implies, it's like watercress but you don't grow it in water. It takes about two months to mature from sowing, likes shade in summer or it will run to seed, but any sun it can get in winter, and it likes its feet damp.

You can treat it like an annual, or a catch crop, or leave it where it is to self-sow. Being very low to the ground, the entangled stems and leaves will fill up with grit and soil from the bouncing effects of heavy rain. One answer is to grow it in a trough you can move about, and let it dangle.

Varieties: none.

LEEK, *ALLIUM PORRUM*

What a wonder is the leek, one of the earliest vegetables humankind found out how to cultivate, a hardy, reliable, cheap, easy, pest-free food plant that is delicious when young, middle aged and old. As with the broad bean, its very usefulness, simplicity and lack of fuss made it, for a while, not quite the thing for those who thought highly of themselves. Parkinson notes in his *Paradisus* that the leek was used for soups in the self-denying days of Lent 'and is a great and general feeding in Wales with the vulgar Gentlemen'.

The traditional way with growing leeks is trenching and earthing up, as for celery, and you are more likely to end up with show-bench leeks if you do go to that trouble, especially if you start early in the year under glass. For the kitchen, all that carry on is quite unnecessary.

Sow in a seed tray in March or any time through to June. When your plants are about as thick as a Biro refill and/or about six inches in height, it's time to put them out. A good place is where you have just removed your first potatoes.

You need a dibber. You can make an ergonomic dibber by sharpening the end of an old garden-fork handle or similar, and fitting a sturdy crosspiece a good nine inches from the pointed end. Place point to soil, press down on crosspiece with foot, hole is made without excessive strain.

Leeks want about nine inches each way. Drop a plant into each hole – it doesn't matter whether the leafy bits do or do not poke over the top – and fill the hole with water. In dry weather and/or sandy soil you should give the ground a soaking before you start, to get clean holes without running infill, and go along again in a few days' time with water, otherwise, apart from routine hoeing, you can leave them to their own devices until you want to eat them.

Ah but, there is controversy regarding your seedlings, ready to plant, and their lives thereafter. This is the view of one authority: '[when lifting the seedlings] a certain amount of root damage may occur; to compensate for this, cut off the tips of the leaves.' Another says: 'Plant leeks ... cutting the tops back by a quarter of their length and the roots by about half.'

And another: 'Wait till the leaves come fountaining up from the depths and their tips are pointing down to earth, then gather them together in a bunch and behead them with a knife to shorten the outside leaves by half and the middle ones rather more. In a wet summer they may need three of these "haircuts" to make them grow more stem and less leaf.' And another: 'Cutting back the leaves to half their length when they droop over is very important and if neglected the plants run chiefly to leaf.'

Modern advice never includes these rituals. The Royal Horticultural Society does not recommend any clipping and trimming. Your very own correspondent has conducted scientific trials under laboratory conditions, consisting of cutting some leeks' leaves and roots and not others. Unfortunately, due to variations in individual plants, the demands of the kitchen pot and forgetting which leeks had been trimmed and which were the control group, no conclusion could be reached. Even so, one can't help feeling that there are some tales of old gardening folklore that are neither here nor there.

If you want so-called 'baby' leeks, of the sort that upmarket chefs weep over, put three or four plants in each hole and dig when they're about as thick as the barrel of a fountain pen. If you want granddaddy leeks, select your best plants, make bigger and deeper holes, put a pinch or two of Growmore or similar in the bottom, and water with comfrey liquor. When the plants are well on, slide a six-inch section of cardboard tube or plastic drainpipe over the plant to give you extra blanching.

Varieties: *The Lyon* was highly thought of until superceded in the late nineteenth century by its direct descendant, *Prizetaker*. Where hardiness is paramount, *Musselburgh*, also called *Scotch Flag*, is an older and sturdier favourite. *Bleu de Solaise* est un poireau vénérable that may be even more hardy than *Musselburgh*, and it has more interestingly coloured leaves. Some leeks are classified as earlies, some as lates, but really they all benefit from the longest growing season you can give them.

LETTUCE, *LACTUCA SATIVA*

If you thought that fancy-dan red frilly saladings and other lettuciary novelties were bred recently according to the demands of Messrs Waitrose, Islington branch, think again. Never mind your lollo rossa and your purple mizuna. There's a whole weird and wonderful forgotten world of lettuce for you to explore.

White Paris Cos Lettuce
(⅛ natural size).

If you follow the year-round lettuce routine you should be able to pick one every day. Lettucers of the highest rank will sow a few seeds every fortnight, in different varieties and circumstances according to season and purpose. Those of the middle rank will do something similar and, with a few panes of glass to use as cloches, will have lettuces most of the time from April to October, or longer in genial climes. If you can't be bothered with all that, you can throw a few seeds around in the spring and, despite the best efforts of the slugs and the birds, some lettuces will almost certainly turn in during the summer. All three regimes can be followed using cos or cabbage types.

Let us eat lettuce all year round. Start in February with a sowing of a fast-growing type in the warmth, followed a fortnight later by another, and again with another under glass outside – coldframe or cloche. Plant out your first sowings under protection – cloches or coldframe – when they look strong enough, an inch or two high, say, giving them about six inches of space in rows a foot apart or as convenient for the cloches you happen to have.

Continue with sowings every two or three weeks outdoors without cloches, bearing in mind the birds and the slugs. Your sowings in August will give you lettuces through October and November, so they may need protection against the cold. In September sow winter varieties, and some of the faster types too. With care and nurture, these will keep you going through the short, dark days. Finally, in October/November, sow under glass to give you some early starters to plant out next March.

You may be attacked by lettuce root aphis; the sad, drooping signs are similar to those of cabbage root fly. Affected plants have had their chips – uproot and burn.

Varieties: there are four families: *L. s. capitata*, heading or cabbage types, subdivided into butterhead and crisphead; *crispa*, which are the variegated, sometimes curly, non-heading sorts, mostly to have their leaves picked as and when rather than uprooting the whole plant; *longifolia*, the cos or romaine sorts; and *angustana*, asparagus lettuce also called celtuce, stem lettuce and Chinese lettuce, grown mainly for the stems of its leaves, if at all.

The earliest known types were of the cos family, around 4500BC in Egypt and other civilisation-cradling regions. Pliny the Younger lists several varieties in his *Historia Naturalis*, published in Rome in 77AD, including different colours and the use of the term *crispa*. Oak-leaved, red-spotted and curly types were all known in Renaissance Europe and were taken to the Americas by the first Europeans to go there. Now there are hundreds of strains, but if that's not enough, the Greater Prickly Lettuce, *Lactuca virosa*, grows wild in limestone areas, especially near the coast, and is reasonably pleasant to eat.

Little Gem, a cos/cabbage-type cross from the late nineteenth century, is the one to use wherever rapid growth is required. *Winter Density* is a good, all-season cos type. *Webb's Wonderful*, early 1800s, is a big, big crisphead favourite. *Lobjoit's Green* cos, from the mid eighteenth century, is sometimes grown by the aficionado under a glass bell-jar. Failing bell-jars, allotmenteers might tie up some of their *Lobjoit* with loose elastic bands or string, to get a crisper, more blanched inside. *White Paris* is similar. *Tom Thumb* is a small, general-purpose one from the late 1700s, developed from those butterhead strains called tennis ball, because of their small, tight heads. You can still get *Golden Tennis Ball*, also called *Gotte's White Seeded*. They don't over-winter but, like *Little Gem*, will do well otherwise for those who don't want to get too involved and would rather not be overwhelmed by huge lettuces. *May King*, from the early, 1900s is another rapid grower, with pinkish edges to its leaves. *Stanstead Park* over-winters well.

Bath Brown Cos was a Victorian essential, a variety from the previous century that would stand through the winter with protection and could be forced and blanched. It actually has green leaves, if a little greyish, with a red-brown tinge, and it can still be had – not to be confused with *Dutch Brown*, also a very hardy, old variety but a small, loose-headed cabbage type. *White Cutting* is a come-again *crispa*.

The type seen in every book and on every list from the late 1700s onwards is *Imperial*. While writers are complimentary, they variously describe it as a winter-hardy cos, a summer butterhead and more. This seems to be an example of giving the same name to different varieties, which is the opposite to the usual breeders' practice of giving new names to the same variety, thus claiming it as their own. Today's *Winter Imperial* is a winter-hardy butterhead.

If all that is not confusing enough, in America when lettuce growers say *Imperial* they mean the lettuces our supermarkets call iceberg, named for its money-saving comfort in cold storage and not, as you might think, because it has about as much flavour as an ice cube. Howsomever, the true *Iceberg* is the lettuce previously known as *Batavia Blonde* or *White Silesian*, a solid, crisphead type indeed but with red tinges to its leaves. It was mentioned by European authorities in the eighteenth century and by the great W Atlee

Burpee at the end of the next. His modern catalogue gives 1894 as its introduction, although the strain offered today is the chillable supermarket one, not the one the founder described thus: 'There is no handsomer or more solid Lettuce ... strikingly beautiful.'

A nineteenth-century American gardener, Charles Dudley Warner, said 'Lettuce is like conversation: it must be fresh and crisp, so sparkling that you scarcely notice the bitter in it.' He was talking about raw, salad-bowl lettuce, of course, but what about the cooked form? Mr Heston Blumenthal, the man who put PhD chemistry into cooking, wrote an article in a magazine about how to make paper hats for use when braising lettuce. You put the hats over the lettuce, not on your head, but your correspondent would suggest forswearing the millinery on the grounds that life is short enough already, and using a pan lid, were you ever to braise a lettuce.

BOILED LETTUCE

... from a 1920's book of cookery and household management.

Trim off the green outside leaves from a large lettuce. Wash the heart well, then tie round with a piece of tape. Put it into a saucepan of boiling salted water (one dessertspoon of salt to each quart of water), boil quickly, until tender – from 20 to 30 minutes. Lift the lettuce out carefully, drain well, and remove the tapes. Cut it in half lengthways, then across, and lay it in a hot vegetable dish. Pour melted butter sauce over, and serve with buttered toast. Lettuces are really excellent served in this way, but only the bleached hearts must be used. Lettuce may also be stewed and served with a brown gravy.

'What?' you say, as if boiled lettuce hearts were not enough. 'Brown gravy?' Read on.

LETTUCES, MRS B?

These form one of the principal ingredients of summer salads. They are seldom served any other way, but may be stewed and sent to table in a good brown gravy flavoured with lemon juice.

Mrs Beeton kindly supplies the method for brown gravy, should you be gasping to try out this way with lettuce. It takes four hours to make half a pint.

Brown about half a pound of cheap beef, a little bacon and half an onion in dripping, add a pint and a half of water and a clove, season, and simmer for the aforementioned time. Melt a knob of butter in a saucepan, add a little flour, and stir in what's left of your beef stock.

And now, to give your dinner guests that special treat, put some stewed lettuces in a warm tureen, pour the gravy over and squeeze half a lemon thereon.

MARROW AND COURGETTE, *CUCURBITO PEPO OVIFERA*

The traditional place to grow marrows is on a manure heap. Where there is no manure, the half-rotted compost heap will do just as well and may even be better. The messages here, even if you don't have heaps, are moisture and plenty of raw, uncivilised feeding material. The plants need a goodly pocket of proper soil to get going, say a foot in diameter and a foot deep, but beyond that let the roots wander where they will. Beside each pocket, which should be spaced four feet from the next marrow, two feet from the next courgette, ram in a length of drainpipe to help you direct water and liquid fertiliser in quantity right to the roots, or a plant pot will do the same job.

At each pocket water well, and put in three or four seeds, pointy end down, not deep – just covered is fine. Over them place a jam jar or other transparent miniature greenhouse. When the plants are threatening to throw off their jars, remove same and the weakest seedlings, leaving only one at each station. Surround it with a thick ring of soot or soot and lime, and/or place a slug trap nearby.

The only thing left to do, apart from routine maintenance including lots of watering, is to decapitate the main shoot when it's two or three feet long. This will encourage side shoots and therefore fruit.

Marrows are like young birds in the nest. The bigger, stronger ones get most of the sustenance. Depending on your disposition, you can either pick the larger ones for the table and thus give the smaller ones a chance, or take the

'We were first informed of its good qualities by Mrs Elizabeth Hubbard, a very worthy lady, through whom we obtained seed from Captain Martin. As the squash, up to this time, had no specific name to designate it from other varieties my father termed it Hubbard Squash.' **Mr James J H Gregory,** *Magazine of Horticulture,* **December 1857.**

Hubbard Squash (⅛ natural size).

littlies as mini courgettes and devote all your prayers to Mr Universe in the middle, or more properly Mrs Universe seeing as it's the female flowers that give birth. Keep any big ones off the ground in some way, with a brick or a piece of wood for example, but not so as to give shelter to a family of slugs.

Come the autumn you may want to store some of your marrows, rather than making marrow jam, marrow rum and so on. They will store quite well if you stop them bleeding. The old-fashioned way of doing this is thus: cut your marrow from the plant at the point where the stem goes thin, and dip the cut end in molten sealing wax. In view of the difficulty and expense involved in obtaining sealing wax these days, you may wish to reinterpret this traditional method in terms of what you might have in your shed by way of sealants. An additional precaution is to keep your new-cut marrows somewhere warm and dry for a few days to tan the skins, as it were, before putting them somewhere dry and cool. If all this works, keep some of the seeds of the last and ripest one for planting next year.

Varieties: 'To my thinking by far the best Marrow is the *Cocozelle*, which most folk so appreciate it is served in the leading continental hotels.' 'Those who like marrows about them that are fat and such as Swell o' Nights should ignore the small bush kind and grow *Long Green Trailing* whose offspring so often rides in state by perambulator to village flower-show victories.' And who is your correspondent, to argue with Mrs Sinclair Rohde or Lawrence D Hills?

The one described in G Thorburn's Seeds catalogue of 1824 as Vegetable Marrow is clearly the one we call *White Bush*, the small, marrow-shaped squash with white skin, eaten whole when a few inches long and, if left, growing not much larger than a foot. At least, it would do that if you could get it, which you can, in Canada. In the UK you can find *Long White Bush*, a larger derivative that you can eat as small as you like. This one has the advantage of being easily visible, as does *Burpee's Golden*.

MARROW GLACÉ

Peel, deseed and cut into sugar-lump sized cubes a ripe marrow or several marrows, giving you about three pounds of fruit. Soak overnight in water, and drain. Sprinkle a pound of white sugar over the cubes and leave for the day, then add two more pounds of sugar, the juice and grated rind of two lemons, and two teaspoons of ground ginger – or more, if you're gingery and lemony. Leave overnight, while the marrow gives forth liquid.

Cook the whole lot gently until the marrow cubes become translucent and the syrup is nice and thick. Now you can follow two routes. Bottle your preserve as it is in jam jars, or put some or all of it in a bowl, cover, and leave for a week. Drain it of its syrup and let the cubes dry somewhere warm on a rack. Mix a pound of caster sugar with half a teaspoon each of bicarbonate of soda and cream of tartar, and roll your cubes in it. They will store well in greaseproof paper in a tin. You could experiment by adding a few pieces of beetroot to the cooking, to make pink Marrow Delight.

MASTERCHEF PUMPKIN

Here's the wonderful Mr Francatelli again, or is it Nigella?

I am aware that pumpkins are not generally grown in this country as an article of food for the poorer classes, and more is the pity, for they require but little trouble to rear, and yield an abundance of nutritious and cooling food, at a small cost; the chief reason for the short supply is, I imagine, the want of knowledge for turning the pumpkin to good account as an article of food. I am now about to supply easy instruction to convey that knowledge to whomsoever may stand in need of it.

Your correspondent's chief reason for not adding to the supply of pumpkins is that very abundance of which Mr F speaks. Once upon a time, bereft of any notion of how to turn a particularly large specimen to good account, it was taken to the cricket club dinner and donated as a raffle prize. The fellow who won it was at the tennis club lunch the following day and, generously, he gave his pumpkin prize to their raffle. Unfortunately, he won it again. Taking it home in an understandably emotional state, he left it in the porch. Early next morning, setting out to walk the dog, he fell over it and broke his ankle.

If only he had had the benefit of Mr Francatelli's knowledge, he might have sliced up a generous quantity of his golden globe and set it to boil in water with some butter until reduced to a pulp, added half a pint of skimmed milk 'to every person who is to partake of the porridge', seasoned it with salt and a little nutmeg, and served it 'with toasted bread for breakfast or any other meal'.

ONION, *ALLIUM CEPA*

Decisions, decisions. Is it worth growing ordinary cooking onions when they're so cheap in the shops all year round? If it is, the simplest way is to grow from sets, but that's non-traditional being largely a post-war phenomenon, sets earlier having had a reputation for bolting and for being the resort of the lazy gardener. Also with sets, you will not be able to plant the more interesting old varieties. But, is it worth going through all the palaver of growing from seed? Probably not if all you want is plain cooking onions, but the shop onions might have been sprayed with all sorts of …

Heat-treated onion sets offer just about the easiest route to grow-your-own anything, apart possibly from garlic. Stick 'em in the ground in March a few inches apart so the top is just submerged, go along the row again the next week to replant the ones the birds have pulled out, and that's it. You will have onions. The more you hoe and the more deeply cultivated your soil the better; water as necessary, fertilise, and you will have many excellent onions. If you do nothing at all, you will still have onions.

Letting your onions dry and ripen in the sun seems to help them keep better, and certainly your correspondent would deem it an essential part of the shallot-pickling process.

The non-set way, with seed, is to sow in open ground or in a nursery bed in March; earlier and/or under glass if looking for really big onions. The problem is the seedlings, which are tiny, like little green hairs bent over, and they are very difficult to keep weed-free. Also, if they're sown where they're to grow they'll need thinning, which brings the dreaded onion fly. If they're to be transplanted, they will still seem much more attractive to this pest than sets, which have no fly trouble.

Sowing in late summer/early autumn risks losses from frost. You want the little onions to grow sufficiently to have the strength to stand the winter, but not so much that their too-large bulbs freeze and die.

One answer is autumn sowing in seed trays or pots, if you are able to provide cool protection in an unheated greenhouse, coldframe or conservatory. Harden off the seedlings as soon as you can on the milder days of early spring and, come March, you should have the equivalent of your very own onion sets. You can follow this same autumnal procedure for salad onions, only you'll eat some and plant out the rest.

Having pulled onions at will during the summer, using the greens as well as the young bulbs, you will come towards harvest with your crop going brown. A walnut-skinned allotment ancient is bound to tell you to bend over your onion leaves. This, you will be told, is to redirect the onions' ripening energy away from the leaves and back into the bulbs, thus rendering you more likely to stay well be-onioned through winter.

Scientific experiments conducted in laboratory conditions, consisting of bending over the leaves of one row of onions while telling the other row not to worry, produced no observable differences. If you want to bend over, fine. You would rather not offend the ancient in question. Howsomever, the onion is doing what comes naturally. It is preparing itself to stand there over the cold, short days, fully resourced in its bulb, ready to send up its flower when the days grow longer again. Possibly, the onion knows what it is doing.

A classic example of onion bending.

Bent or not, frustrate your onions' procreative ambitions by lifting them and drying them off before hanging them up to store. Some authorities recommend a two-stage ripening: a lift half-clear of the soil with a fork in expectation of a dry spell of weather, followed by completion of lifting and a thorough drying in sunshine or shed. Now, for each six or eight onions, from which you have rubbed any loose skin and dried soil (if you want to; some idle folk never bother), take a piece of string with a loop knotted in each end. Pass the string around the corporate neck of the bunch of onions, put Loop A through Loop B and hang Loop A from a nail. You can now withdraw an onion without disturbing the others, because your hanging noose automatically tightens. Next year, you will be surprised and delighted to find your onion strings still hanging there, ready.

Varieties: the alderman of sets is the French-bred *Sturon*, and very good it is too. In seed, *Bedfordshire Champion* and *Ailsa Craig*, both from the latter half of the nineteenth century, are firm favourites with those who want the aforementioned plain cooking onion but with scope for special treatment to give magnificently glowing and very large showbench specimens. Many of the earlier-bred types belong either to the white- or silver-skinned line, or the red line. *Paris Silverskin*, also called *White Egyptian*, is from the beginnings of the nineteenth century and can be picked small and delicate, and *White Lisbon*, usually grown as a salad type but making bulbs if left, predates that. *St Thomas's Onion* may be easier to say than *Braunschweiger Dunkelblutrote* (the Darkest Blood Red of

Brunswick) but it's the same thing, an old red variety that keeps well. A female allotmenteer seeking a partner in life may peel one of St Thomas's onions and place it under her pillow, preferably wrapped in silk. While she sleeps, a vision of the desired one will appear to her in dreams. It may work for males too. Or not.

The giant of them all is *The Kelsae*, the *Guinness Book of Records* onion at over fifteen pounds, about seven and a half kilos. One onion, over a stone in weight and almost a yard around, could hardly have been envisaged by Messrs Laing and Mather of Kelso when they introduced *The Kelsae* in the early 1950s. They would have been proud enough of Mr S C Hill of Galasheils when he held the Guinness record in 1985 at 7lb 6oz (3.4k). Your correspondent once witnessed a recently harvested crop of these onions, hanging up in a shed, having been grown in the walled garden of a Kelso hotel. It was an awe-inspiring sight. *The Kelsae* is a mild-tasting beast and not a good keeper, but my, is it big.

The *Tree onion*, *A. c. proliferum*, sometimes also called *Egyptian onion*, is more a curiosity than anything. It looks like a cross between chives and an Arizona cactus, producing a cluster of little onions, about the size of commercial pickled silverskins, on the top of its stem around two feet above the ground. This cluster sends out shoots curving upwards to produce more clusters, hence the cactus-tree effect. You can propagate by planting the little bulbs in the early spring but they won't give you anything until the following year. Proponents of this variety might call the onions it produces 'mild'. We might call them virtually tasteless. If you have chives and proper onions and/or shallots, the *Tree onion* can only be grown for a laugh, which is a good enough reason.

SHALLOT, *A. ASCALONICUM*

First-rate, really crisp and powerful pickled onions are impossible to obtain in any shop, and so the pickler's only true course is the shallot. This type of onion is increasingly appearing in fancy recipes, too. Your correspondent buys growing stocks from the greengrocer or market stall, looking for the semi-flat-sided, non-spherical type. Cultivation is exactly as for onion sets but they can go in sooner and grow more like garlic, setting clusters from the one planted. The biggest and best are saved for next year's planting, if you remember and/or can resist pickling them.

The secrets of superb pickles are twofold: drying and ripening the shallots before splitting them, and giving them a good strong brining for a few days after peeling. Your commercial onion pickler does neither of these things. He just takes them from the field, peels them and puts them in coarse, poorly spiced vinegar, which is why they are soft and so, well, vinegary.

Peeling is best done under water (the shallots, that is, not the peeling person). Pour several kettles of very hot water on to your quarry in a big vessel and peel when you can get your hands in. Your hands will smell of onions for days afterwards but you won't cry so much. Make your brine allowing a good pound of cooking salt to a gallon of water. Leave the onions in it for several days.

Having grown your shallots, ripened them and brined them, and the peeling was the worst bit, you will want a full reward for your labours. Vinegar comes in half litres these days; everything else comes in spoons or can be counted.

To each half litre of good-quality but not costly vinegar – own-label white wine vinegar is ideal – add a dessertspoon of white sugar, half a teaspoon of powdered cinnamon, a teaspoon of powdered ginger, ten whole cloves, twenty peppercorns (preferably black and white mixed), five allspice berries, and twenty dried chillies. Your correspondent also adds a half teaspoon of Cayenne pepper and/or more chillies.

Bring this liquor just to boiling point and immediately pour into a mixing bowl or similar wide and rapidly cooling vessel. Pour the liquor over your shallots when cold, distributing the spicy debris equally between jars. If you do this in due season with the window open, every wasp for miles around will come and see you. Do not be tempted to add herbs, unless you like vivid green onions.

PARSNIP, *PASTINACA SATIVA*

Use new seed every year and place three or four at each spot, about nine inches apart, in March/April. They take a long time to germinate, anything up to three weeks, which makes life difficult for weeding. Lawrence D Hills suggests sowing radishes between parsnip stations, which are up in a few days and so help you know where things are.

When the snips do show, give them a few days then thin to one per station as soon as you can see which is the big brother. Beyond general maintenance, that's it, although

if you want to grow some really big ones it pays to help them out. Using a metal rod or other stout pole, make a conical hole as deep as you like, fill it with potting compost and ram it firm. Sow your seeds in that, thin out as before, and amaze your friends. Conical holes can of course be made and filled when nobody is looking.

Parsnips are very hardy and can be left until you want them. Pre-frost, they may taste rather starchy; the cold weather produces a reaction in the root, changing starches into sugars. Because the seeds don't keep, and because they're so prolific and easy, and because you are not growing an F1 hybrid, after the first frost identify a couple of your finest snips and reserve them for seeding.

Varieties: oldest and best is *Hollow Crown*, from the early nineteenth century. Also very good are the mid nineteenth *Tender and True* and *The Student*, the latter possibly edging it in colder districts and when it comes to size. All are excellent in flavour. Newer varieties may claim better resistance to canker, which is a fungal infection that gets into cracks in the roots. With proper soil cultivation you shouldn't be getting canker anyway, and later sowings should avoid cracking, and therefore canker, altogether.

WE BREWED

... some small beer today.
We had Peas for the first time out of our Garden.

The Diary of a Country Parson, James Woodforde, June 28th, 1787

PEA, *PISUM SATIVUM*

The modern argument over peas, whether it's worth growing your own when the frozen ones are so good, can easily be resolved if you have a couple of smallish children handy. Ask them to pod some peas from your allotment while you go and do something else. When you return there will be a heap of empty pods, sure enough, but where will the peas be? Not many will have made it as far as the pan. QED.

Peas need help. Mice attack the seeds. Slugs and birds attack the seedlings and you

can't blame them. Pea shoots are every bit as nice to eat as the bean shoots in your chicken chow mein. Unless they are of the dwarfest varieties, peas also need support, to get going upwards and to hold on to when they are up there.

They're greedy too, so need lots of nutrients, but they are nitrogen fixers like all legumes, so they will leave you something in return in their roots.

One way to defeat the mice, the slugs, and birds to an extent, is to sow indoors or in the coldframe. A normal seed tray is really too shallow; pots are better to contain the long, feathery roots. Peas will transplant quite happily. Folk see nothing wrong with buying sweet-pea plants six inches high so what's wrong with edible-pea plants? Nothing.

In the olden days BCB (Before Clarence Birdseye), devoted gardeners would seek the holy grail of peas through the year, with autumn sowings coming in under glass in the early spring, three sowings of first earlies in

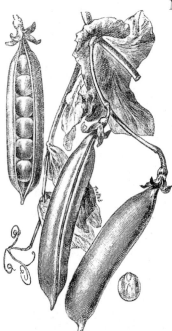

Vilmorin, the major French breeder and grower founded in 1742, developed this sumptuous-looking marrowfat pea in 1936.

March and April, two sowings of maincrop in April/May and another of a slow grower in May, with two more of the fastest growing in June/July. If you can be bothered with all that, well and good. Peas to cook with the new potatoes, peas to have raw with summer salads, and some mangetout – that seems like a good enough target for your correspondent.

In any case, peas like lime, wood ash and last year's manure, and plenty of moisture for their roots. Put seeds or plants about two inches apart in double rows with about eighteen inches between, with space between the double rows equal to the height the plants will attain. If you are likely to suffer from mice taking your seeds, the old method was to soak them for a day in paraffin, then dust them with red lead. Alf Tupper, the Tough of the Track in the old *Rover* comic, used to spray red lead on the insides of industrial boilers in the morning, eat five lots of fish and chips for lunch and then break the four-minute mile, but you wouldn't want to mess about with red lead. Anyway, there's no need. Mice, like all wild mammals, do not like the smell of any petroleum or coal-tar product. Soak the seeds in paraffin and forget the red lead, or soak strips of cloth in Jeyes Fluid, sump oil or, indeed, paraffin, and lay them in a *cordon sanitaire* around your peas but not on top of them. When questioned by the European Tar Police, you can honestly say you are not contravening the law, because you are not using these things 'on plants'.

Most protection against birds is needed when the plants are small, and anti-bird weaponry is easily made. You can buy small-mesh wire netting at just the right size – 13mm mesh in a roll 300mm wide, or half an inch by a foot as we wrinklies used to say. Bend lengths of this into tunnels, pin down with old wire tent pegs or similar, block up the ends with pieces of mesh or glass, and your happy uncle is Robert. Spend a little more time tacking the edges of your wire to wood, such as tile battens, and you have long-lasting, storable anti-bird furniture that can be redeployed with ease as the omega of defence.

Once the plants are about to power through the wire mesh, take it off and, unless you are growing dwarves, insert supports, being careful not to thrust through the pea roots. The classic first-phase support is everywhere described as brushy hazel twigs but you may not have access to hazel. Anyway, it wants to be brushy, with taller canes or other support added at the same time if you have found a tall type you want to grow. The canes should be higher than the stated height of the variety which, in the case of the more modern ones, is seldom over three feet. Or, you can grow them up netting. It's only common sense, really.

A small handful of dried marrowfat peas from the healthfood shop.

Varieties: although one of the very earliest cultivated vegetables, peas were largely a field crop until the late 1400s. Before, and for many years after, they were left until sare and threshed as dried peas to be fed to cattle and people, the younger green seeds being too bitter to eat. Probably the most famous and long-lasting of these medieval field peas, derived from the wild plant *Pisum arvensum*, is the *Rouncival Pea*, so called not because it came from the Spanish village of Roncesvalles but because some monks did. They, of the order of St Mary of Roncesvalles, had a hospital in fifteenth-century London, at Charing Cross, where they developed this pea. And, you can still get it. Nowadays it's called the *Maple Pea* by the few farmers who grow it, and pigeon pea or carlin by certain sections of society in northern England. Carlins, otherwise generally thought of as pigeon food, are soaked and boiled for eating on the fifth Sunday of Lent, the one before Palm Sunday, hence the little *aide memoire* for good Sunday scholars: 'Tid, Mid, Misere, Carlin, Palm and Paste Egg Day'.

Anyway, should you want to grow the *Rouncival Pea* you will need to seek out a farmer or agricultural merchant and ask for *Maple*, or go into a food shop with a sense of tradition. The last time your correspondent saw the carlin for sale was in Penrith Co-op.

The marrowfat style of pea is the successor to the rouncivals, although a *Large Red Rouncival* was still being listed in 1800, after the marrowfats had become popular.

—Feed Your Late Peas. Superphosphate of lime is the manure to use. At this season you cannot fill the pods unless you feed every three days with this manure. If you water-in each application (1oz. per yard run of drill) you will have the pleasure of green Peas as long as fairly good weather holds out.

*   *   *

WHITHER YOUR PEA? (1)

The first food-freezing factories in Britain opened in Wisbech – Smedley's, 1937 – and Great Yarmouth – Birdseye, 1945. Demand from the populace was barely discernable, largely because hardly anyone had the means to keep frozen food frozen. Until those dates and for many years afterwards, one of four things happened to peas commercially grown.

Some went to Covent Garden and other wholesale markets in their pods, to be forwarded to your local greengrocer. The rest had to be preserved somehow at the short harvest time. Some were canned fresh, to be sold in small tins as wrinkly dinky 'Garden Peas'. The rest were dried.

People bought them like that, steeped them and made mushy peas while, over the year at their leisure, the factories also rehydrated the same product and canned it, or made it into pea and ham soup.

Dried, rehydrated, cooked peas come out brown and a problem arose in 1925 when the government banned the use of copper salts to make them green. Scientists soon came back with the answer – sodium bicarbonate and green dye – and more development resulted in the Processed Marrowfat Pea, dried, soaked with bicarb, sweetened, coloured, cooked in the tin. Like the tinned versions of corned beef, tomato soup and spaghetti, the processed pea became a food that had no exact equivalent in nature.

WHITHER YOUR PEA? (2)

Take old peson and boyle hom in gode flesh broth that bacon is soden in, then take hom and bray hom in a morter and temper hom wyth the broth and strayn hom thrugh a strayner and do hom in the pot ande let hom boyle. Serve forth wyth bacon.

This recipe, quoted by Dorothy Hartley in her magnificent book *Food in England*, shows several characteristics we don't see nowadays. Some modern readers, not having done Chaucer at school, might not know that 'soden' is the past tense of the verb to seethe, to cook in liquid. Few modern readers will be used to seeing recipes that give no quantities, and most will not be used to the recipe-giver crediting them with any common sense.

So, take your old peas and boil 'em up in strong meat broth, that is to say, the water you boiled your bacon in. When they're done, smash 'em up in a mortar and make the result suitable for straining by adding broth. Strain and, if it seems necessary, reduce by giving 'em another boil up.

A dish of peas with bacon has been delighting people since it was possible, and not only because of its savour. Using expensive and scarce animal protein to flavour vegetables to their mutual benefit is nothing more than sound household practice.

Edward Lear is said to have developed the word into 'runcible' as both a type of hat and of spoon, although quite what that has to do with anything, goodness knows.

Marrowfats today seem to be obtainable only from agricultural merchants and in varieties suitable for commercial farming, although the variety *Senator* is a direct descendant and a good substitute. The simplest method is to extract a handful from a packet of dried marrowfat peas in February or March, soak overnight and plant under a couple of inches of compost in shed or coldframe. Some brands of pea may have been heat-treated and so will not grow. Scientific experiments under laboratory conditions have not been conducted across the whole range of brands but thirty peas from a healthfood shop, given the above treatment, produced well over two-thirds germinations.

It is probable that the Italians were the first to breed a pea to be eaten fresh and green. It was tiny and delicate compared to the large, butch and peasantish field type. They called it the New Pea, *Pisello Novello*, and took it to France where royalty and nobility fell in love with it and called it the Small Pea, *Petit Pois*. The rest, as they say, is history.

Prince Albert, early nineteenth century, is reckoned to be among the sprinters, six weeks from sowing to picking in favourable circumstances, and *Little Marvel*, a superior strain of *American Wonder*, *circa* 1900, is even quicker. *Kelvedon Wonder* from the 1920s is still a favourite. For a bigger, slower grower, that is to say old-fashioned maincrop, *Ne Plus Ultra* (nothing more beyond) comes from the late nineteenth century and is still available, unlike so many of the older, tall varieties. Champions of the past such as *Gladstone*, *Kent Blue* and *Lancashire Lad* are now on the endangered list and pleading for adoption. You can still find two from the late nineteenth century that grow over five feet high, *Alderman* and *Tall Telephone*, sometimes shown as the same variety while other merchants differentiate.

POTATO, *SOLANUM TUBEROSUM*

'These potatoes be the most delicate roots that may be eaten, and doe farre exceed our passeneps or carets.' This was written around 1598, about specimens of *Ipomoea batatas*, the sweet potato, a South American import first brought to England by John Hawkins in 1564. It needs a nice comfy climate to grow in, with lots of water at 75°F (24°C) minimum, so that probably won't work on your allotment, whereas a plate of pigeon-egg sized, new *Solanum tuberosum,* straight from allotment to pan, certainly will. And then you can say 'See'st thou here, O beloved one, how I doe provide for thee the most delicate roots that may be eaten, which doe farre exceed even your organic Charlottes from Tescoe.'

It is not reliably known how and when the potato we came to know so well arrived in Britain. Sir Walter Raleigh did have it planted on his Irish estate in the late 1580s but there is no evidence that he brought it over. The most likely route is from Peru via the new colony in Virginia. The Spanish had it first and it is also possible that Irish

A nice crop of delicate roots that will keep this chap going until the Last Trump sounds.

beachcombers found potatoes among the wreckage of the Armada in 1588. Whatever the true story, the potato was not an immediate hit. It wasn't until the 1750s that its potential for feeding the masses was properly realised in mainland Britain, although by then it was long established as a staple in Ireland.

A gentleman with a heart called John Forster in 1664 published a book 'for the good of the poorer sort', with the rather snappy title of *England's Happiness Increased or A Sure and Easy Remedy Against all Succeeding Dear Years: by a Plantation of the Roots called Potatoes.* In this work he set out how, with the support of King Charles II, the potato would set the world to rights. 'But when these Roots shall come into use, People will live more happily and plentifully, Trading will flourish, and much Glory will redound to Almighty God, for discovering so profitable a Secret.' Alas, John Forster got nowhere and the potato stayed unpopular. A seedsman's catalogue of 1787 lists twelve varieties of runner bean, ten of pea, thirteen of cabbage, seventeen of lettuce and only six of potato.

There was a terrible grain harvest in 1794, with attendant rise in the price of bread to a shilling and fivepence a loaf, about £3.50 cash equivalent today, but, taking into account a poor man's wage then and what it would buy, a shilling and fivepence was more like the whole amount a family had to spend on food for a week. At last, the nation was more or less forced into being persuaded that spuds 'r' us.

The potato is a bountiful crop, a great multiplier, giving manifold returns for little effort, and so is relatively cheap in the shops. The allotmenteer must consider whether limited space is best occupied by maincrop potatoes for winter storage, or whether to go exclusively or mainly for the unparalleled delights of the new.

The method is the same for both. Buy your seed potatoes in February and set them out in seed trays or any kind of shallow box, rose-end up, in plenty of light and no heat. The rose end is the end with the eyes; the other end just has a flimsy little remnant of where it used to be joined to the plant. These eyes will sprout, or chit, into small green miniatures of a potato plant. An ancient authority on your allotment site will tell you to rub off all but two or three of these shootlings. Thank him, and maybe even promise to do so, but don't bother if you're going for new. The effect of rubbing off is to give you fewer but larger spuds.

The earlies will be ready to go in in March, the maincrop at the beginning of April. Take out a trench of a spade's depth and quarter fill it with manure if you have it, comfrey leaves and best compost from your composting system. Add a thin layer of soil and set your seed potatoes thereon, firmly and with the sprouts pointing up, a foot apart (your foot) for earlies, a foot and a half for maincrop. Gently fill in with loose soil so as not to damage the sprouts. The soil remaining will come in for the earthing up, which you will do as the leaves appear if there is danger of frost, or when they're about six inches up if not. Give them another earthing at another six inches, leaving a couple of inches poking out. That should be it, except for keeping the weeds down until the plants have grown to weed-smothering dimensions. Strewing more comfrey between the rows can only help matters.

Start digging when the flowers appear but are not yet open. Yes, the spuds are small but they are wonderful to eat, and by the time you get to the end of the row they'll be the size of cricket balls and bigger.

The great enemy of potatoes, especially maincrop left in the ground all summer, is blight, and particularly so on allotments where it can spread easily. The evidence is clear: your leaves go brown, wither to a crisp and die. It is a fungus, also affecting tomatoes. It thrives in warm, wet weather, is borne on the wind and the rain, and it can attack the leaves and the tubers both. So, for instance, if there are unseen spores on your leaves and you water from above, you are sending the spores into the soil, so don't. Good earthing up will help protect against invasion by water. Spraying the leaves with a copper-based fungicide, when earthing up is complete, will help prevent but is no remedy if the infection is already in. Bordeaux mixture – one part copper sulphate, one part slaked (hydrated) lime, one hundred parts water – is the traditional spray for this job, and the traditional time for doing it is the first week in July. You might like to do it a little before.

Your earlies are less liable to get blight, simply because of when they are grown. If you do get it, burn all affected leaves and stems. The spores live through the winter on unconsidered bits of potato and plant haulm, underground or in your compost heap, so good housekeeping is essential.

Varieties: different varieties of potato have different degrees of resistance to the dreaded blight and, wouldn't you know it, some of the very best eating types are among the most susceptible. The list of blight bunnies includes *Epicure*, *Golden Wonder*, *Kerr's Pink* and *Majestic*. The fairly modern variety *Cara* shows good blight resistance and, traditional or no, we have to point to a recent development, the arrival in the UK of the *Sarpo* potato cultivars such as *Mira* and *Axona*. Bred in Hungary, these are the nearest thing so far to blight immunity.

Pink Fir Apple, pre-1850, is a salad potato that also is marvellous hot as new. Early and best for flavour is *Epicure*, *circa* 1900. The extra flavour may be the reason why slugs don't like them so much. Good second earlies are *British Queen* and the one famously known as Jersey Royal which, confusingly, is a variety called *International Kidney*, nineteenth century, and not the equally good Scottish one called *Royal Kidney*, 1899.

For maincrop, try *Kerr's Pink*. A good all-rounder and keeper is *Majestic*. Not as heavy cropping as some but generally voted best tasting is *Golden Wonder*, *circa* 1900. Of course, there's nothing to stop you digging up your *Golden Wonder* when they're small, as new potatoes, is there?

NO VEGETABLE IS

... or ever was, applied to such a variety of uses in the North of England as the potatoe; it is a constant standing dish, at every meal, breakfast excepted.

Sir Frederick Eden, *The State of the Poor*, 1797.

RADISH, *RAPHANUS SATIVUS*

You don't need to make a lot of fuss over radishes. Assuming your plot is well cultivated, they'll grow pretty well anywhere and can be sown pretty well any time, even in winter in mild regions. They shoot up and mature quickly, twenty days from sowing to eating in good weather – which is why they make a good catch crop while you're waiting for something else to grow.

Sow thinly, of course, and pull them when they're ready. Don't leave them to stand unless you want pods for a pickle and/or seeds to save. The most likely pest is flea beetle, which can reduce the foliage to lace but not usually before the radish is ready anyway.

Varieties: some are hot, some are not, and some are from China, whence several authorities state the cultivated version originated. Whether it did or no, it's certainly one of our oldest friends and its name is witness to that, meaning simply 'the root', from the

Latin *radix* via the Anglo-Saxon *rædic* and not, as often believed, anything to do with it being red. Indeed, among the most venerable strains are the *Black Spanish Round* and *Long*, sixteenth-century types, and *Long White Icicle* of the same era. The first mentioned is a very good all-rounder, hardy, with an excellent peppery taste, although not so quick growing as some. All the *Icicle* strains are milder tasting. *Chinese Rose* is another large, winter-hardy, flavourful one from the early nineteenth century, all of which rather makes the classic red and white *French Breakfast*, 1865, something of an interloper. Two very speedy, reasonably peppery, late-nineteenth-century types are *Sparkler* and *Scarlet Globe*.

R. s. caudatus, the Rat-Tailed Radish, has no root worth talking about but enormous seed pods, sometimes a foot long. It may not be traditional in UK allotments but they know all about it in Asia, where the hot pickles come from. Seed may be hard to find, but found it can be.

They grew and ate this in 1550, and you can still get it.

RADISH POD PICKLE

Let some radishes run to seed and pick the pods when the seeds are there but before the pods get tough. Boil up some fairly strong brine, put in your pods and turn off the heat. When cold, the pods should be bright green. If not, give them the treatment again. Take them out, rinse, taste for saltiness, rinse again if necessary, and pack in a glass jar with something contrasting in colour — mild red chillies, sprigs of cauliflower blanched and brined — and top up with distilled or clear wine vinegar and a few peppercorns. This is an adaptation of a recipe from Dorothy Hartley.

SALSIFY, *TRAGOPOGON PORRIFOLIUM*

This is one of those vegetables frequently described as rare, unusual, and why don't we grow it more often. If a veg is rare and unusual, in many cases there is a very good reason, but not so with salsify, also called oyster plant. It is pest free, trouble free, hardy, easy to grow, and it tastes very good in a subtle sort of way. One drawback possibly is that in heavy ground it tends to produce skinny roots and poor rewards. One answer is to pull the prize parsnip trick and make deep conical holes filled with potting compost. The other drawback has no answer; it is hairy and mucky with soil and so provides extra preparatory work on the way to the plate, compared with parsnips and carrots.

Sow in March/April where they are to stand, thin to a foot apart, and that's it. Start digging them up when they look ready, October time. If you leave roots to over-winter and you don't dig them all, you will have a bonus in spring of shoots that you can pick and use for salad or cooking greens, or you can earth the shoots up, which blanches them, to cut and use like asparagus. If you don't eat them all, flowers something like purple dandelions (same family, *Compositae*) will result on tall stalks, that is, if you haven't picked them at the bud stage, steamed them and eaten them with mayo. Your very last salsify, left alone, will go to seed like a big dandelion clock.

Still, the main purpose is the roots, hairy, twisted and forked though they may be. Cook them skin-on, peel and deal with them quickly, in a sauce or lemon juice or whatever, because they will go grey as fast as look at you.

Varieties: *Sandwich Island* is the traditional, nineteenth-century one, sometimes called *Mammoth*.

SCORZONERA, *SCORZONERA HISPANICA*

Another of the why-don't-we-grow-its, and there is a reason this time. Although described by writers of old as being utterly delicious, they didn't have to deal with it. They had servants. Easy to grow it may be, like salsify, but to prepare and cook those long thin black roots, even thinner than salsify, is an unrewarding experience. First you have to get the undernourishing sticklets out of the ground without them breaking. Getting the soil off by scrubbing is the next job, then you steam them with the skin on, then you peel them, and then you wonder what all the fuss was about.

The flavour is, however, appreciated by those whose diet is restricted in some way. There exist brave persons of the vegan persuasion who would discuss, with wine-buff enthusiasm, the subtle differences between the components of a feast made entirely with scorzonera, salsify, kohl rabi, calabrese stems, skirret and scolymus, while others would find the subject somewhat arcane.

Scolymus, by the way, *Scolymus hispanicus*, with the glorious German name of *Goldwurzel* that we call golden thistle and Spanish oyster, used to be cultivated in the UK for its roots but seed no longer seems to be available except in the wild.

One redeeming feature of scorzonera is its ability to thicken up over the next year. The plants will shoot and flower like salsify – these bits also are edible – but, unlike other similar crops, the roots will stay in good condition through a second summer.

Varieties: *Noir de Russie* or *Giant Black Russian* is the one you can get fairly easily, the term 'giant' doubtless referring to length rather than breadth. It is probably a very old type, presumably because nurserymen have not thought it worthwhile to try to improve it.

SEAKALE, *CRAMBE MARITIMA*

Strictly a perennial but it is dealt with here because cultivation is an annual ritual. Classified everywhere as rare, unusual, connoisseur, gourmet and so on, there is no mystery about seakale unless you are a competitive Victorian throwback and want to serve this springtime veg as a most unseasonal Christmas canapé. 'Oh, really, don't you know seakale? I find the flavour somewhere between cauliflower, kohl rabi and asparagus. Protected in the wild now, but Jeremy/Jennifer grows it on the allotment and forces it in elephant dung from the zoo.'

Seeds are available but the usual way to this very fine spring crop is through buying roots, which are called thongs and are sold only in March. Make holes with your dibber about a foot and a half apart, thrust in your thongs so the tops are a good inch below the surface, cover with soil and wait. If a thong produceth shoots, rather than a single shoot, pick off the weaker-looking ones. Ordinary maintenance is all that is now required, although drenchings with comfrey water will be appreciated.

As with chicory, the plant you see is not the one you want. When the white flowers have gone (some authorities say you should not allow flowers to develop) and the foliage has begun to die back – end of October or after the first hard frost, whichever comes the sooner – dig up your plants. Cut off the leaves for the compost heap, and snip off the roots from the main stem. These are your thongs for next year. When snipping, if you want to be traditional, cut from the stem to give the thong a flat top, then cut again about six inches down on the slant, so you'll know which way up they go. Store them in sand or dry potting compost. Give them a damping and a little warm-up in February, ready to start again in March.

Meanwhile, replant your rootless stems in pots of light soil and place a similar pot over the top with its drainage holes covered. No light must enter. Leave these double-potted delicacies in a shed or cold greenhouse and, come the early spring, you will have your reward of tender, gourmet-pleasing shoots to be treated like asparagus. If Christmas is on your mind, keep your plants in a warmer place; the ideal temperature is the same as that for a pub's beer cellar, 54°F (12°C). Or, cover your pots out of doors with a heap of fresh manure or manure mixed with newly fallen leaves, and the heat of their rotting will be your force.

You can forget the digging up and just force your plants where they are in the ground, either by the pot method, as with rhubarb, or by earthing up. If the latter, the earth must be very light as the shoots will not make their way through cold, heavy soil. The drawback with this less labour-intensive method is diminishing returns from your plants in their permanent site. Seakale enthusiasts might combine the methods, digging up some plants for new thongs and some not, forcing some with warmth and some not, so that they can be having their seakale and eating it from December to April.

Varieties: whatever you can get. Varieties mentioned in older texts include *Lily White* and *Purple Tipped*. You can still get *Lily White* as seed, meaning you're three years away from your crop but with an opportunity to become a unique beneficiary to other allotmenteers for, as Keats almost said, 'Where are the thongs of Spring?' 'In France' would seem to be the answer, the French variety *Angers* being the most easily obtainable as thongs in the UK. Traditional, hand-thrown, terracotta seakale-forcing pots can be bought new, and they're only ninety quid.

SPINACH, *SPINACEA OLERACEA* var. *GLABRA* and *SPINOSA*

Lawrence D Hills has it about right when he says 'the spinach secret is either to sow plenty or none at all', meaning that the summer sort, *glabra*, is quick to mature and even quicker to run to seed. Spinach lovers must make frequent sowings and croppings if they are to have their hearts' desire. Others might say 'grow spinach beet instead, it's a damned sight easier'.

Both summer and winter (*spinosa*) types need attention. The former likes lots of manure or compost, and moisture; the latter does not like its feet wet and so is best grown on ridges if your soil is heavy. Place the seeds about three inches apart, expecting to thin one in two. January sowings under protection will yield in April, March in May *et cetera et cetera*, to your last effort in late August with a winter spinach. *Spinosa* has multiple seeds so expect more thinning. These winter ones are pick-and-come-again; go along the row taking some from several plants. In theory, the summer kind is the same except if you pick, when you come again it will have gone to seed.

There is a disease called spinach mildew, which is carried by the weed fat hen. Hoeing should sort that out.

Varieties: there are very, very few traditional varieties in the mainstream catalogues. Search elsewhere and you will find *Viroflay Giant*, a big nineteenth-century all-rounder, but that's about all. Most of them have gone. Where is *Victoria*? Whither *Long Standing Prickly*? *Bloomsdale Long Standing* is a 1920s summer type said to be less liable to bolt. Of uncertain date but qualifying as 'heirloom' and 'heritage', or old, is *Giant Winter*, also *Gigante d'Inverno*, which is, as it says, large in winter but, being Italian, not entirely hardy, so protect from frost.

SUMMER SALSA WALTZER

Chop up some tomatoes and a courgette quite small, also a summer onion, including the greens. Stir together equal amounts of soy sauce, white wine vinegar, Thai hot chilli sauce and soft brown sugar. Mix all in a bowl. When your correspondent first made this, after a surge of creative thought lasting over a minute, the quantity was expected to keep a few days in the fridge but it was all eaten first go.

TOMATO, *LYCOPERSICUM ESCULENTUM*

Despite its reputation as an aphrodisiac and its alternative name of Love Apple, the tomato took a long time to become established as a common and desirable food in the Anglo-Saxon world, both old and new. It came from South America to Europe sometime in the sixteenth century but stayed around the Mediterranean, presumably because it wouldn't really grow in Nordic climes. Also it was red, which northern Europeans thought inappropriate for a food, and many held it to be poisonous anyway, a belief which stayed in some British minds until late in the nineteenth century.

By the middle of that century, Europeans had taken the tomato back to America and the good citizens of the USA, previously suspicious, were going for it in a big way. In more conservative Britain, without the benefit of so many immigrant Italians, the gentry thought of it only as an ornamental plant, the fruits of which could, at a pinch, if you didn't think them toxic, be used to make soup.

Now, of course, tomatoes are everywhere and in everything, and there are hundreds of varieties and all sorts of mysteries surrounding their cultivation. This need not be the case.

Tomatoes are from a warm but not tropical region. They certainly don't like the cold and will not germinate, grow or ripen if the temperature drops below 60°F (16°C). They will die instantly in a frost, but they don't like it too hot either. Once we get into the high 80s F (high 20s C), things are getting a bit much. The ideal would be a constant 72/73°F (22/23°C).

Toms take about four months from seed to fruit in suitable, reasonably consistent conditions, but translate their temperature requirements into a British summer with its cool evenings, sometimes cold nights and sometimes quite unpleasant days. You can clearly see that tomatoes grown outdoors will need a start in the warm if they are to have time to bear and ripen through all kinds of weather and before it starts getting chilly again. Even so, given a fairly decent summer, we should be all right with the appropriate variety, assuming we have a coldframe or some other method of protecting the young plants from the worst of the spring weather.

Of all things that the allotmenteer can grow, the tomato is possibly the one with most potential for improvement over the supermarket version. Although head-office tomato buyers have lately realised that size, shape and colour aren't everything, their suppliers in Morocco or wherever still have to pick their toms green and still have to grow commercially productive varieties. Your toms, picked when ripe, cannot be matched that way.

Your best ground for the job is south facing, by a fence or wall for shelter. Dig a trench a spade's depth. You will be planting at about two-foot intervals, so work out how many you will have and give them a bucket of compost each, plus comfrey leaves, before you fill in. Now, how do you get your plants?

Work out the date of the last possible frost and, four weeks before that date, sow your seeds in damp potting compost in a seed tray, cover with a carrier bag and place in the airing cupboard. If you live where frost is not really a consideration, do this in March. Check every day and as soon as the plants are up, put the tray without bag on a warm windowsill. Don't leave them long enough in this situation to get leggy. Transplant into pots, one little one each or several to a bigger one, when they have a pair of proper leaves. Put the pots in the coldframe.

When the plants are about four inches high, start opening the coldframe during the day. Do this for a week or so, by which time all danger of really cold weather should be past and you can plant out above the aforementioned trench. Keep well watered, and you're on your way to unsurpassable toms.

The easiest ones to grow are the bush types, which need no special measures. The 'indeterminate', that is side-shooting types (see varieties below), need to be trained up canes and supported, and you need to pinch out those side shoots, which grow when you're not looking in the upturned armpits of the plant. See, where the plant has made a good strong branch? In there, between branch and trunk as it were, a little stem with two leaves is showing. Pinch it out now because, if you don't, next week it will be a foot long and sapping energy from your fruiting system.

Once your plant has made four or five good branches with fruit trusses, or maybe six in the mildest regions if it's not getting late, pinch out the top so it can't make any more. Even so, you will end up in the autumn with some green tomatoes and very little likelihood of temperatures rising usefully above 60°F (16°C). Any looking yellowish should be picked on a dry day, keeping their little brackets on, and ripened in a bowl on the kitchen table.

In well-cultivated soil and following good rotation practice, outdoor toms should suffer no pest or disease they cannot deal with, the possible exception being blight (same as potato blight) in a warm, wet season. Spray Bordeaux mixture or similar as a preventative.

Varieties: the original style of tomato was a crawling, spreading, rambling sort of a plant, sending out shoots all over the place. It bore its fruit sprawled out on the ground until some bright spark thought of tying it up to a stick. The other, easier sort is the one we call 'determinate', which is to say self-limiting, not liable to ramble and not in need of support or side shoot pinching. Another name is 'bush'. There are so many varieties, ancient and modern, of both types, not to mention the in-between ones called semi-determinate, which need support but not pinching, that we are compelled to restrict ourselves to a very few. Once we start being indeterminate in our traditional recommendations, we shall need pinching of our side shoots and so be lost.

Of the outdoor bush types, try *The Amateur* and, for cherry toms, *Gardener's Delight*. Outdoors with stakes and good support, go with the late nineteenth-century *Harbinger*, fruit not so big as some but they will ripen well most years.

ON THE PRESERVATION OF TOMATOES

This is an activity for high summer, not for the usual preserving season. At that late time, while you're drying your haricots and pickling your shallots, you will have green tomatoes, not red ones.

Green toms may ripen successfully if you hang the whole plant up somewhere warm, otherwise they almost certainly will not, at least, not well enough for you to want to preserve them. Putting some in a bowl on the kitchen table with a ripe one among them sometimes works although, not having conducted statistically significant scientific experiments under laboratory conditions with and without a ripe tom, one cannot be sure it makes a difference. Wrapping each one in tissue or cloth, with its stalk still on and keeping in a drawer may work too, because the fruit will be less liable in the dark to lose moisture and so wrinkle rather than ripen. Perhaps chutney and piccalilli offer a better answer.

The best way to have your own ripe red tomatoes through winter is to preserve them while you have a surplus, when they are turning in thick and fast. The old-fashioned way is bottling. Either fill your sterile jars with washed toms and top up with a weak, sweetened brine (two pints water to one teaspoon salt and one of sugar), or skin your toms (pour on boiling water, count ten, plunge in cold water, peel), sprinkle with salt and sugar and ram them into your jars, leaving no space. Both now need to be cooked, which scientifically means bringing slowly to bug-killing temperature and holding there for thirty minutes. Domestically it means simmering in a big pan of water, with the jars on a trivet or something to keep their bottoms off the pan bottom.

Next they must be sealed. You can screw on the lid of a Kilner jar or of a jam jar, or you could flip the spring on those French jars, or you could pour candlewax, mutton fat or similar.

If you think that's an awful lot of trouble, you can put your toms on a tray in the freezer, not touching, and throw all the resulting snooker balls in a carrier bag for fishing out at will, for cooking, obviously.

Or, you can do it the Italian way. Boil up your toms with salt and basil leaves until you have a mush that will go through a mouli, and you have passata, which freezes well. It freezes just as well as a plain mush without the mouli.

Or, dry them in the oven. Immerse your toms in olive oil – leave cherry toms whole, cut larger ones in half – lift out, drain, and arrange in a single layer on a baking tray. Sprinkle with salt and bake in a slow, slow oven for several hours, until they are as dried as you want them to be. Pack them in jars in the same oil and they will keep, but not forever.

TURNIP AND SWEDE, *BRASSICA RAPA* and *B. NAPOBRASSICA*

Why turnips are comical and carrots are not is a matter for speculation, but this fine and important vegetable remains a synonym for twit, especially rural twit. Turnip Townshend, a viscount, old Etonian and MA (Cantab), government minister and international diplomat, ended his days in 1738 as a figure of fun because he developed

a four-year system of crop rotation. It revolutionised British agriculture but it featured turnips, and therefore was amusing.

Swedes need half a year to full maturity, so if you want big ones, sow early under glass and hope for a summer without drought. Anyway, your allotment swedes will be a revelation if you have only known the shrink-wrapped bowling woods they sell in the shops. Some turnip types are very quick growing – sow in April and pull in June – and all offer early greens from their thinnings that come in handy when there is little else. Sow some in early March under glass for cropping in May. There is no special trick in growing them. Like all the brassica family they like a firm start; sow at one-inch intervals and firm the row by treading a plank or whacking with the back of your spade. Thin gradually to about six inches apart for the quick small ones and a foot for the big wintery ones.

In theory, being brassica family, turnips and swedes are vulnerable to clubroot and root fly. In practice, because you will have limed your soil, you won't get clubroot. The fly seldom attacks, leaving you with flea beetle and maybe powdery mildew, but really you should not be unduly bothered.

Varieties: the classic swede is the *Purple Top*, also called *Champion*. In turnips, *Milan Purple Top*, *Jersey Navet* and *Snowball* are all nineteenth-century strains for the first earlies; *Jersey Navet*, also called *Vertus*, grows long rather than round. For winter use, the hardy *Manchester Market* – mid nineteenth century – is good.

Herbs

The ideal way to make a herb garden would be to make little beds designed on decorative lines with perhaps a sundial and a seat. Such a garden could well be made near the kitchen quarters, particularly in any household where domestic help is employed. If so designed as to give privacy, and furnished as suggested with a seat, the herb garden would make an ideal resting place for the staff.

Also, Mr M James FRHS might have added, it would be ideal for the allotmenteer who, in quiet moments, might well want to continue philosophical researches, have a crafty smoke and/or glass of something, or just listen to the bees and smell the smells of summer.

The main culinary herbs are trouble free except they mostly need to be kept in check. They self-sow all over the place – chives, parsley, bronze fennel – or grow well beyond the bounds you set – mint and lovage, for example. The perennial shrubby types such as rosemary, thyme and sage are relatively well behaved, although tarragon is not as hardy as might be needed in some parts. There is little point in buying packets of hundreds of seeds for most of these; buy a plant at the market, unless you want to set up as a herb-plant supplier yourself.

Some should be grown from and for seed, such as coriander, which bolts for any reason at all so, if you want to use the leaves, follow the spinach secret. Mustard is another. Your correspondent, at that time living in Norfolk, took a fancy at outdoing Mr Colman of Norwich and grew a fine crop of mustard. Having judged that the seed was about ready to gather, he was called away. Returning the next fine morn with eager pot, he found that the pods had opened, the wind had blown and mustard seed was scattered to all corners. The small quantity of seed that could be gleaned made one small jar of a feeble, mild and undistinguished condiment. More research needed.

Basil, that is the Italian sweet basil, is possibly the one slightly troublesome herb that

MOCK TURTLE SOUP WITH HERBS

Turtle meat was all the rage in Regency times and to serve it was living proof that you were (a) very wealthy and (b) well up with Mrs Fitzherbert. Those lesser folk, who could not afford to pay for a turtle imported live from the Cayman Islands, naturally tried to produce something like it from cheap and easily obtained ingredients.

Take a large calf's head and ... No? But you do need meat that will give you a gelatinous texture. Hide, bones and cartilage produce a liquid which will set into jelly when cold. That's the sort of thing. Here's a modern translation.

Take some or all of: breast of lamb on the bone, pig's trotters, beef rib bones, chicken carcase. Make a goodly panful of stock. Strain. Shred into it some mutton very small (ideally, or lamb) and some lean, well flavoured beef such as shin or skirt. Add half a bottle of Madeira or cream sherry (well, it is supposed to be a luxury). Add the herbs from your allotment, a good handful torn into shreds of thyme and/or basil and/or marjoram. Add two onions minced through the fine plate, or blitzed if you don't have a Spong, and/or a couple of leeks, the peel of a lemon grated, and pepper. Instead of salt, add a few shakes of Thai fish sauce, *liquamen* or *garum* (see next page). Simmer until it's done, check seasoning.

The correct way to serve it is over slices of hard-boiled egg or with little forcemeat balls. Whether or not this turns out closely resembling your actual turtle soup, your correspondent wouldn't know, never having eaten the real thing.

is really worth growing. You have to treat it as a tender annual and either keep it indoors in a pot except in the finest weather, or plant it out when summer is thoroughly on the go, but fresh basil is a wonderful thing. Should you have difficulty, you could go to the rather extreme lengths of Keats's fourteenth-century Florentine stunner Isabella, whose lover was murdered by her brothers. She found the body and cut off the head, which she placed in a garden pot. Filling it up with compost, she put in a basil plant, 'And so she ever fed it with thin tears / Whence thick, and green, and beautiful it grew.' No, no, no need for that. A sprinkle of Growmore will do.

If you want to go in for herbs in a big and detailed way, you should get hold of a copy of *Classic Herbs*, published by Remember When and written by your faithful correspondent.

ROMAN RELISH

This is something to make in the latish summer, when your herb garden is in full production and the right kind of fish are in season.

Take a quantity of strongly flavoured, oily fresh fish – sardines, herrings, pilchards, mackerel, anchovies, sprats – in any combination, whole. Wash them and smash them to a pulp.

In a crock or plastic box, put a layer of big, powerful herbs – mint, lovage, coriander, basil, anything really. Use the stalks and all. Lovage, *Levisticum officinale*, is also known as *liebstöckel*, which translates as 'love stick' or 'love plantlet', but nobody seems to know why. Anyway, it was widely used by the Romans. Put a layer of mashed fish on the herbs, then a thick layer of salt, another layer of herbs, fish, salt, and so on. This is going to stink, so put it somewhere out of the way, well protected against flies but not sealed. After a week give it a stir, then stir daily for another three weeks. It should now offer you a runny thickish sauce, ready to sieve and put in sealed jars. The correct Roman jar, or amphora, held almost eight gallons, which you may think is rather a lot.

Alternatively, go to the oriental supermarket, get a bottle of *nam pla* and some tins of anchovies, mix with your herbs chopped up and allow to macerate for a few days. The Romans made two types, called *liquamen* (fish relish thin) and *garum* (fish relish thick).

If you're going to cook *in modo Romano*, you will also need *defritum*, which is a thick general-purpose sweet sauce made by boiling down very young wine (must) with added honey, to about a third of its original volume. This is an ideal use for homemade wine from allotment surpluses, for example, of rhubarb. Several versions of defritum were made with varying degrees of sweetness and concentration – *caroenum*, *passum* and so on. Fig syrup is often given as an equivalent but those readers of a certain age, who remember being dosed with California Syrup of Figs whether they were constipated or not, may wish to use the real thing.

WINTER SAVORY

Satureia montana is a bushy, perennial herb, easily grown, with many uses. The Romans chopped it up with vinegar to make a sauce, as we might make mint sauce. Its flowers being so aromatic, they also liked it to grow near their beehives. Later cooks mixed it dried with breadcrumbs to make their fish fingers. One of its active ingredients, carvacrol, has antibacterial properties, which may be why, without knowing the science, its use was so universally recommended when ingredients were not always perfectly fresh.

The great herbalist Nicholas Culpepper offered apposite and up-to-date advice in his book of 1653: 'The juice [of winter savory] mixed with oil of Roses and dropped in the ears removes noise and singing.' Now, there's a thing. Culpepper, thou should'st be living at this hour, on the number 43 bus. Removes noise and singing. You can also make it up into a poultice-type paste with flour, which may ease 'palsied members'.

Glasshouse Annuals

CUCUMBER

Here we have part of a family that embraces the watermelon and the loofah, which are as widely cultivated in the UK as the pineapple and the tamarind. Of all things you are likely to grow, the cucumber is among the most demanding and, one might add, the one with the least point. Only three and a half per cent of a cucumber is not water; food value, almost zero. The big, greenhouse, non-pickling types do not keep but all turn in, not quite at once but through a short season. They are cheap in the shops, and the ones you grow do not taste significantly better in your salmon sandwich. Regardless of which, there is something deeply satisfying in watching a cucumber lengthen and seeing it hanging there in glory.

The first problem is heat. Cues like it hot, more than tomatoes, and F1 hybrids (see below) want even more warmth than traditional types. Cues will not germinate below 60°F (15°C), or 68°F (20°C) for F1s, and they expect you to keep them at 75°F (24°C) during the day. If you cannot maintain these temperatures, you are in for a big struggle with scant recompense – 'maintain' being the operative word. They like it warm all the time, but not too hot. A greenhouse with no shading on a hot day will kill them as surely as Jack Frost nipping at their noses. They also want lots of food and lots of water, and you have to give them something to climb up, plus more support if they bring forth in manifold fashion.

A problem with traditional varieties is that they bear two types of flower, male and female, although, in the unisex world of the cucumber, the male is unnecessary. In fact, he's worse than that. You do not want the male flowers mating with the females because, if they do, your cues will be so bitter as to be inedible. She's the one with the miniature fruit behind her. He looks the same but has no fruit. Pinch him off before he can do any damage. This task assumes regular and frequent attendance at your greenhouse. In the mainstream catalogues, almost all varieties offered are F1 hybrids, expensive, non-traditional, but with the advantage of never or very rarely bearing male flowers.

Varieties: the only one you will see in the big-name catalogues that is not an F1 hybrid is *Telegraph Improved*, and that is because so many gardeners want to grow it. This is a mid nineteenth-century type, from *Rollinson's Telegraph*; you can also get the slightly later development, *Perfection*.

PEPPER, SWEET and CHILLI, *CAPSICUM ANNUUM*

Well, yes, you can grow these outdoors in the mildest regions but they stop operating below 70°F (21°C), need high-ish humidity and a long season, and like acidic soil. They may not have been a common crop on allotments in the past but they have been around for hundreds of years and so can count as classical. The sweet and the hot require the same regime: sow near the beginning of March under glass, or earlier in the warmth, and transplant when you have sturdy-looking seedlings. You want a bushy sort of habit so it can be a good idea to pinch out the top of the main stem once the plants have grown big enough and are well established.

A good friend of your correspondent, who lived by the coast of east Devon, used to grow all manner of chillies from seeds filched on foreign holidays. She sowed and grew on in a warm conservatory and only put her much-prized and potted plants outside for the best three months of the Devonian summer. She always maintained that the degree of hotness in the flavour of the chilli depended on the weather; the warmer the summer, the hotter the chilli.

Having tried to grow chillies outdoors through a miserable, cold and wet summer in Norfolk, with half a dozen fruit resulting that were a tenth of the size of their parrot-food forebears (see below) and had no flavour whatsoever, of heat or anything else, the writer's experience seems to confirm this belief. If you do live in warmer climes, the outdoors will prevent attack by whitefly and red spider mite, which can be a serious pest in the greenhouse.

Although everywhere discussed and treated as annuals, some chillies will develop into a woody bush that will flower and fruit for several seasons, even if cruelly treated, so long as the cruelty doesn't go as far as frost. This is known from experience to be true of the *Habanero* and *Scotch Bonnet*, also of a nameless Turkish type got from the Devon friend, that grows upwards from the branch. When dried, this seems to match the *kirmizi biber* (Turkish for red pepper, boringly) that is sold salted and smoked in gourmet shops.

Varieties: for sweet peppers, big and early is the *Spanish Mammoth*, dating from the mid nineteenth century. Another sweet one, of the longer sort, is *Dolce de Bergamo*. *Long Red Cayenne* is a very old strain, sixteenth century, but not the same species, being *C. Frustescens*, not that it makes any difference to cultivation. *Jalapeño* and *Habanero*, named for Xalapa in Mexico and Havana in Cuba, are widely available.

Growing plants from shop-bought dried chillies probably won't work because they are likely to have been oven dried. If you can get fully ripe chillies at the market, you can dry them yourself and many, many seeds will result for little outlay. Similarly, you can find large, bonnet-type chillies in the pet shop, in parrot food, and these will germinate because nobody spends money on fuel to dry parrot food. Parrots, incidentally, have no saliva, which is why they can eat chilli seeds without blinking.

CHILLI OIL

Once upon a time, having a surprisingly large crop of chillies and hearing a Portuguese barman called Jose talk about using chilli oil on barbecued meat, your correspondent decided to ask how this, then novel, condiment might be made. Having listened carefully, meanwhile noting that chilli oil was also good as a dip and a salad dressing, a jar was filled with fresh chilli pods and the magic mix was poured up to the top, being one part extra virgin olive oil to one part Scotch whisky.

After a month or so, guests at a luncheon voted overwhelmingly in favour of the oil, exclaiming at its power and energising effect. Subsequent conversations with the Portuguese barman in question revealed something lost in translation. The real recipe was one part extra virgin olive oil, one part Scotch whisky and eight parts sunflower oil.

TOMATO

Sowing is the same as for outdoor types, except earlier, and if your greenhouse stands on open earth, cultivation is pretty similar too except you are only growing indeterminates and you have the option of strings hanging from the greenhouse roof instead of canes or stakes. Your flowers will need pollinating and insects may take care

If tomatoes are soaked in boiling water before being peeled the skins will be more easily removed.

Always make sure you put some water in the kettle first.

of this but, just to be sure, give your plants a little shake now and then, or a blow over with a feather duster.

Toms need plenty of food and water, but too much food can persuade them to go more for foliage than fruit. Some authorities advise removal of leaves to help get the light in, even though no plant likes having its leaves removed. If you find yourself doing this in a green jungle, don't over-feed next time and bear in mind that while your toms need light to grow, it is air temperature that ripens them, not sunlight.

If your greenhouse has a solid floor, or even if it hasn't, you might consider a method, now unfashionable, called ring culture. Your correspondent tried this in a conservatory and it worked very well. It's a two part system. You build a kind of rectangular sandpit, filled with sand and gravel, mixed, and preferably fitted with a drainage tube/channel, and you keep the sand/gravel moist. On to it you put your toms, planted in large pots with incomplete bottoms. Ask for whalehide pots at the garden centre (no, of course they're not real whale), or remove most of the bottom from any large plastic pot, and fill with a good rich soil. The plant puts its feeding roots around the pot and its drinking roots down into the sandpit.

There is a balance to strike. The sand must always be damp but never flooded. The toms want feeding but too much liquid manure will seep into the sand and start up a whole new ecosystem, probably a smelly one.

Indoors, there seem to be more enemies than outside. They are the same enemies but your friends the predators and the fresh air do not have free access to conduct business on your behalf. Chief among enemies is the allotmenteer who waters irregularly, causing the toms to split, or provides insufficient calcium in the soil, causing blossom end rot, or lets the greenhouse get too hot and stuffy, causing leaf mould and red spider mite. Ah me and lack a day. And you might get whitefly, which is a sod to get rid of. One way

Tomatoes being grown indoors using a variant of the old-style ring culture.

is by hanging old-fashioned fly papers above the tomato plants. Shake the plant, the whitefly decamp upwards, and bingo. Yellow fly papers also work because whitefly are attracted to that colour, and you can make your own sticky trap by painting a board thickly, every morning, with bright yellow gloss. It is traditional to start doing this on the first day of April. Another way is to spray with fairy oil (see page 140).

Varieties: in the unheated greenhouse you can grow any of the outdoor ones plus those that will grow outside but really prefer indoors, such as *Ailsa Craig* and, for something different, the yellow-fruited *Golden Sunrise* developed around 1890. *Chadwick's Cherry* is prolific as well as strong on flavour. *Imperial* is, as you might expect, a good old 'un, and it is not impossible to find.

ALL THAT GROW

... in the country about London, cabbages, radishes, and spinnage, being impregnated with the smoke of sea-coal, which fills the atmosphere of that town, have a very disagreeable taste. I ate nothing good of this sort in London, but some asparagus.

Pierre Jean Grosley, *A Tour to London*, 1772

Perennials

ASPARAGUS, *ASPARAGUS OFFICINALIS*

Patience is a virtue, and one much needed when setting out towards asparagus. If you are very, very patient you can grow it from seed; otherwise the usual method is to buy established plants, a year old, called crowns, that look like large, white, dead spiders. From these you will get nothing for a year, then a little the following year, then a lot for the next ten or twenty years. The bind, though, is not so much the wait as the preparation of the bed. It needs to be fertile, well drained, absolutely free of weeds, and deep. If you have heavy ground with a lot of clay, either don't bother or make a raised bed, adding drainage lighteners to the soil.

The classic method is to make a bed three feet wide, so you can reach to cut your spears without treading on it, and three spits deep, so you begin by digging an experimental hole of three spade lengths. If you hit clay, give up and go raised. If not, continue digging a trench of the stated proportions and as long as you like. At the bottom put gravel, broken bricks and so on for drainage, and as much manure,

Asparagus Delight.

1 bundle asparagus.   Salt.
Water.   Tomato slices.
Green peas.   Lettuce.

Scrape the white part of the asparagus stems, beginning from the head. Tie them in bundles of 20, keeping all the heads in one direction. Cut the stalks evenly and keep the asparagus in cold water until it is time to cook it. Have ready a saucepan of boiling water, add a heaped teaspoonful of salt to each quart of water, put in the asparagus, and boil gently for 20 minutes. Serve on a bed of crisp lettuce leaves and garnish with tomato slices and cooked green peas.

Recipes like this make you realise how worthwhile it is to go to all that trouble.

compost, leaf mould and whatnot as you can provide, plus a sprinkle of lime and, if you can get it, seaweed. Asparagus grows wild by the coast, especially where the ground is sandy, so a sprinkle of salt will help too. Continue enriching the soil with those things as you fill back your trench, making sure that you remove every shred of ground elder, couch grass or anything else that looks like a root. In effect, you are making a giant seed bed.

A good time to do this is in the summer, when you should be relaxing and watching your other plants grow. All the perennial weeds you have missed in the bed will have a chance to shine through and be seized, and many of the annual weeds can germinate and be hoed, because hoeing will be difficult once your crowns are in. If you can arrange it, and if you have the necessary fowl, running a few chickens over the bed for a week or two will weed it and fertilise it.

Come the spring, you need to be ready for the arrival of the crowns you have ordered. They don't want to be left lying around to dry out. So, when they come, look at your dead spiders. The stem in the middle needs to end up about three inches under the soil, while the legs should spread and dangle down a little. Across the length of your bed take out two shallow trenches, about six inches in from the edges and a foot between, sufficient to allow the right space for the spiders, which you should place a good foot or slightly more apart. Fill in soil to the top of the stem and later, when you see signs of growth, fill up to the top.

Sprinkle some general fertiliser mixed with a handful of salt over the bed – water-softener salt will do – keep the bed free of weeds, and wait. Do not be tempted to cut anything from the plants until the second year after planting, even if the catalogue says you can. Some authorities recommend staking the first-year stems, as they grow waist high or higher and a strong wind could be disaster for this shallow-rooted delicacy. In any case, cut the stems back to near ground level when they die down in the autumn.

Harvesting, when you get to it at last, is done with a knife, slicing below the soil's surface, taking care not to cut stems you can't see yet. By the end of June or a little later, you should desist to allow the plants to go their way, except for not permitting any berries to mature and fall, thus giving you more weeding to do.

There is a specialised pest, the asparagus beetle, which looks like a small brown ladybird and which lays its eggs while you are in mid cropping. The maggots eat your asparagus.

Varieties: seeds of a mid nineteenth-century type, *Argenteuil Early*, can be had by the very patient, also *Conover's Colossal* of similar vintage. Crowns of the latter can be found, and of an early twentieth-century type, *Mary Washington*. Commercial growers of course go for F1 hybrids.

The mid nineteenth-century variety Vert de Laon, called Large Green Paris in English, has very large heads and the best reputation for flavour, but will not stand cold northern winters.

GLOBE ARTICHOKE, *CYNARA SCOLYMUS*

The only mystery about this crop is why people bother giving permanent houseroom to thistles four feet high and three feet wide that only give you a bit of leaf to dip in butter. Still, if you must, they are best propagated by division in the spring, so beg some from a neighbour or buy some plants. Don't take any heads in the first year unless it's been an especially good growing season, in which case a few can be had late on.

Varieties: the usual one is the imaginatively named *Green Globe*, and you can get them in purple.

HORSERADISH, *ARMORACIA RUSTICANA*

The main problem with horseradish is not how to grow it but how to get rid of it. It obviously does better in good soil, although most allotment holders would confine it to an unlovely spot, which is why they get skinny roots. The leaves are all right for salad when young and tender, and you can dig up a root whenever you want, take some, put the rest back like a fish and one day, unless you are a horseradish fiend, you will decide to dig it all up and put something else in, like more rhubarb. Somebody on your allotments is probably doing that right now.

WELSH ONION, *ALLIUM FISTULOSUM*

The Welsh onion or *Ciboule*, in Latin the garlic made of pipes, is a hardy perennial bunching plant more like a leek than an onion, a kind of onion-flavoured lemon grass. It is grown mainly for its leaves as it has no bulbs to speak of, and will produce oniony greens when there is little else about, which is as well as it's not much use otherwise. A red type called *Siberian Everlasting* may be more productive and will certainly stand the winter.

SKIRRET, *SIUM SISARUM*

A sweet, white carrot-style vegetable that grows in bunches like octopus tentacles, skirret has fallen from favour. Once 'the most pleasant of roots' (*Systema Horticulturae*, John Worlidge, 1677) and top of John Parkinson's list, seeds are now only obtainable from heritage specialists. As with scorzonera and salsify, those praising skirret did not have to deal with it in the kitchen. The roots can look not so much like a neat assembly of thin parsnips but more like the tangled mass below a well-established mangrove.

Sow in April or whenever you're sowing your carrots, spinach beet and so on. Thin seedlings to a foot apart. Young shoots can be gathered at will and used as you would bamboo shoots. Roots should be ready to dig in September. Splitting and replanting the roots is the way forward from that point.

This is a very hardy perennial, which can grow six feet tall or more. Leave the roots in the ground until needed. You should not be troubled by any pests, which will be too surprised by seeing skirret to attack it. Similarly, no celebrity chef will be able to tell you how to cook it (do it with the skin on).

This is what skirret looks like above ground. Below ground, it's anybody's guess.

SORREL, *RUMEX SCUTATUS*

This excellent perennial will grow virtually anywhere and is normally propagated by splitting the roots, so maybe one of your fellows on the allotments has some. Otherwise, you can grow it from seed but you only want three or four plants at the most. If you see flowers forming, pinch them off or the plant will think its job is done for the season.

A sharply interesting addition to the salad bowl, and an early one, sorrel is also very good used where you might otherwise use chives, such as with cream cheese. You can make a sauce with it for use with white meats like veal or chicken. The method is the same as for mint sauce: shred and chop sorrel finely, pour on a little boiling water, add sugar and vinegar when the sorrel has infused. You can cook it like spinach, which is to say hardly at all, with no more water than two dewdrops and a knob of butter and, if you add a good chicken or turkey stock to that, you have a fine soup.

RHUBARB, *RHEUM RHAPONTICUM*

The best rhubarb your correspondent ever grew was the result of an accident. Walking with the dog and the wife one spring day across some scrubland, it was realised that this was no ordinary common but abandoned allotments. There were straggly, gnarled old currant bushes, and goosegog bushes, and rhubarb. In need of the latter, a spade and a sack were taken there next day and a large slice was stolen from that rhubarb plant that had rested in peace for many a year. The slice was like a lump of wet, yellow wood, about the size and weight of an old Littlewoods catalogue. It was dropped in a manured hole, covered with more manure, and it grew and it grew and it grew. Advice about not picking first season sticks was disregarded and majestic, superb rhubarb was effortlessly produced for evermore.

Some of it was used to make pink champagne, following the *méthode champenoise* of the elderflower. A five-gallon barrel of this was provided at a general election party when the party of the red flag lost comprehensively to the party of the blue, but all parties of the first, second and third part were unable to report any constipation the next day.

Should you not have abandoned allotments from which to steal, rhubarb crowns are easily obtainable from nurseries. Rhubarb is not fussy about where you put it, within reason. It does like some sun, and it does like muck, and you really shouldn't pull any sticks in the first year if you're growing from a nursery plant, nor should you, when in full swing, pull any late in the season when the plant is reconstituting itself and the sticks may contain rather too much oxalic acid to be palatable or healthy.

This acid gives the leaves additional uses, such as in cleaning up old wood, and it is the reason why folk with gout are generally told not to eat rhubarb. Oxalic acid and milk do not mix because it precipitates calcium as calcium oxalate, the chief constituent of kidney stones, and yet, oddly, rhubarb is frequently served with custard.

Pre-season sticks can be had by forcing, which is nothing more than putting a large crock or galvo bucket over part of the plant, plus a sack or something else to keep the worst of the cold out.

Varieties: *Red Champagne* is an excellent choice. *Victoria* is a late fruiting one, and *Timperley Early* is a good one for forcing.

Fruit

When your correspondent was gardening semi-professionally, that is, supplying produce for breakfasts and dinners at the farmhouse B&B being run by his beloved and himself, a truth about soft fruit was manifested. When the gardener is under pressure of time and unable to spend all the hours that are really necessary, raspberries and blackcurrants show themselves to be the winners out of the soft fruit class. They need minimum maintenance for maximum reward.

Each year the blackcurrant crop was processed thus: a large quantity of carefully selected prize specimens was frozen on trays, after sprinkling with sugar so they could be bagged in a reasonable state of semi-separateness. The rest, without topping or tailing and without necessarily removing every leaf and bit of stalk, were boiled up with a little sugar. This great mess of blackcurrants was run through a sieve and the resulting juice-cum-puree was frozen in plastic cups. Each cup represented a year-round recipe opportunity. There was an ice-cream maker. Real blackcurrant ice-cream, made with loads of real cream and real eggs ... well, you can imagine. Well, no, you can't, unless you've had it.

Same thing with raspberries. Freeze a goodly number whole, puree the rest. Wonderful. Of course, strawberries also are wonderful, see below, and must be carefully considered. A large number of gooseberry bushes would have been needed to produce an equivalent to the blackcurrant crop and they're not so versatile in the kitchen. And, they won't forgive you so easily if you fail to prune.

For one reason and another, the blackcurrants – and the redcurrants – were not pruned for two years. This did not stop them from producing masses and masses. Redcurrants also are not quite so versatile nor universally appreciated a fruit as the blacks but they are worth thinking about if you have the room, provided you know the Redcurrant Secret.

You see, on a certain summer's evening, the Blackbird Herald Pursuivant notes that the colour of Mr Farnsworth's ripening redcurrants has changed, from a pale yellowish green to a pale greenish yellow, with a slight, almost imperceptible, hint of pink. The Herald promulgates this news throughout the neighbouring parishes and, next morning, every blackbird in the county assembles at Mr Farnsworth's allotment. The thrushes of the area, having eavesdropped on the Herald Pursuivant, turn up as well. By the time Mr Farnsworth comes downstairs for breakfast, thinking in terms of an allotment visit, his entire crop of redcurrants has been stripped. All he has left are hundreds of empty, dangling, yellowish green strings and a few tiny green currantoids.

Ah, Mr Farnsworth, if only you had kept an eye, like the Herald. When that colour change took place, and it was only a slight change, you should have gathered your redcurrants by the stringful and put them on a sack to ripen in the shed. They would have turned the most beautiful red and you could have made pots of jelly to have with roast lamb, and Cumberland sauce, and oh, so many nice things. Still, you have your blackcurrants left. For some reason, at least in the experience of this writer, birds do not bother with blackcurrants, no matter how ripe. Other growers may disagree.

Three rules for the *Ribes* family, that is currants and gooseberries: plant no closer than four feet apart with room for you to get between rows; mulch in the spring, with muck and compost; feed with potash. And a bit of common sense: obviously the bushes are going to sit there for good, so give them a good start with plenty of future nourishment in the bank.

BLACKCURRANT, *RIBES NIGRUM*

You want your bushes to be a kind of bowl shape, curving up from the base, so when you plant, anytime between October and March, you should look closely at which way the buds on the new shoots are pointing. Cut new shoots back to three or four buds with the uppermost one pointing outwards. Also cut out anything in the middle.

The regime from then on comes in three sizes. Size C is do nothing at all until the bushes are such a tangle that you really have to. Size B is cutting out some of the older wood, that with blackish red bark, to make room for the new, which are shoots with light brown bark. Do this sometime in the winter. Size A is to cut out all the old, having-fruited wood every year, as soon as fruiting is finished, leaving only the new. This regime will result in fewer, but larger, showbench style currants and should avoid the infestation called Big Bud. If you see leaf buds much enlarged in the wintertime, there are mites inside eating them. Pick off the buds and get rid, because the mites carry a very nasty disease called Reversion which will completely do for your blackcurrants.

Varieties: *Seabrook's Black*, from 1913, is an early/mid season type with medium-sized fruits, borne in heavy clusters. It flowers late so should miss the frosts, and it has good resistance to Big Bud. *Boskoop Giant* is very early and so is better for milder areas. *Goliath* is an old one, mid nineteenth century, and big-fruited. Recommended as the largest berry of all and with excellent flavour is *Laxton's Giant*, not so easy to find.

REDCURRANT, WHITECURRANT, *RIBES SATIVUM*

You also want a bowl-shaped bush for these two, which are the same species but in colour variety, but the bowls should stand on a stem. Cut off any shoots that appear close to the ground so that you have a six-inch leg. The other chief difference from blacks is that the reds and whites grow fruit on old wood, not new or, more precisely, the strings of berries hang from junctions between main stems and year-old shoots. You encourage the formation of these shoots by cutting the ends off everything – the main branches where you think the bush is big enough, and the newer side shoots at the third or fourth bud.

Varieties: *Laxtons No 1* and *Redlake* are favourites in red. In white, *White Grape* is the standard.

GOOSEBERRY, *RIBES UVA-CRISPA*

Here the intention also is to make a nice, open, bowl-shaped bush, and on a stem about six inches high. Winter pruning should have this objective, without worrying about whether shoots are from this year or last, but cutting out any branches that are definitely past it which, in most cases, is after four or five seasons of fruit-bearing. Gooseberries like to send crooked, zigzag shoots all over, so that you cannot gather their fruit without being lacerated and, if left, can come to resemble tumbleweed on a stick. Gooseberries also quite like shade and so will flourish where perhaps other plants might not.

Varieties: the all-rounder with the biggest reputation is *Lancashire Lad*, which ripens in red. *Careless* may have no cares for itself but needs more care than other commonly planted types from you, because it wants to spread. An old type now brought back is *Whitesmith*, earlier than some and not fussy about soils.

RASPBERRY, *RUBUS IDAEUS*

The big thing about rasps is that they are very shallow rooting, making weeding with a hoe impossible. So, if you are not prepared to use a weed killer, you must clear the ground completely of perennial weeds before planting, keep on top thereafter with mulching, for instance with lawn mowings, and hand-weed as necessary.

A raspberry cane from the nursery is shaped a little like a golf club, with the hairy root as the head. These roots want to be in the soil no deeper than a couple of inches. It's no help to give them any more

Save the Old Raspberry Canes.

WHEN cutting out the old canes from your Raspberries don't throw them away or burn them.
Trim off all the side-growths and strip off the leaves. Then tie them up in bundles, placing a tie at each end and one in the middle to straighten then.
Store the canes away until next season. You will then find you have some good stakes for your tender-growing plants, which need light support.—(J. Habishaw, Roseacre, 39, Belle Vue Avenue, Roundhay, Leeds.)

roofing and could be a hindrance. They will send up a spray of new canes so anything other than a singular row is a waste. Plant them about fifteen inches apart, or a foot and a heel, stamp them firm and cut the club shaft down to about a foot high.

Now you need to think about support, if you haven't already. Rasps grow shoulder high or higher and will fall over without your assistance. This is usually given with posts at the end of the row, and in the middle if it's a very long row, and wires wrapped around. A wire at thigh height and one at shoulder should do, and you can tie the canes to the wires if you can be bothered. You will have to net your rasps too, against the birds, who love them, so bear that in mind when designing your construction. Higher posts with cross-pieces will make life easier.

Every year you should cut out the canes that have fruited, the brown ones, leaving the ones that grew last season, the green ones, to give you the next crop. Also cut out any spindly, weedy looking green ones because they won't do you any good.

Varieties: many of the old ones, such as *Lloyd George* and *Norfolk Giant*, have been crossed with and subsumed into newer, more disease-resistant types. The East Malling family is possibly the most famous and *Malling Jewel*, first offered in 1949, is widely available and sought after, offspring of *Lloyd George* and others.

Autumn fruiting types are quite different. They bear on this year's growth, rather than last year's, and so are to be cut down every February. They also need less support, if any.

Privately educated brambles flourish beside Scarlet Emperor runners, while that transplanted Swiss chard bolts like mad in the background.

Autumn Bliss is probably the one you want, yet another result of *Lloyd George*'s procreative activity at East Malling, this time with three different species entirely, including an Arctic dwarf and two Americans. For this feat alone, surely it deserves your consideration.

BLACKBERRY, *RUBUS FRUTICOSUS*, and LOGANBERRY, *R. X LOGANOBACCUS*

... also Tayberry, Dingledangleberry, Doodahberry and Whatnotberry. Ever since an American judge called Logan accidentally crossed a raspberry with something, possibly a blackberry/dewberry called *Rubus ursinus*, there have been endless attempts to produce a fruit that rambles like a bramble, tastes a bit like a raspberry, but has gigantic fruit. You may ask what is the point of that, when we already have such excellent rasps and giant blackberries, and the answer might possibly be the complaints one hears about blackberries growing on tayberry plants, or it might be the thornless loganberry, originating in the 1930s and, unlike its prickly forebears, giving you rather nice fruit.

Cultivation of black and logan is the same. Give them plenty of room, such as five or even ten feet between (depending on blackberry variety, see below) and, for logans and the more expansive blackberries, plenty of wires to be tied to, on stout posts. These are not likes rasps, merely leaning and lounging on the support you provide. These are going to weigh heavily on it, and rely on it, so it needs to be strong.

Cut your plants right back after planting before Christmas. Put blackberries anywhere, including shady nooks, but logans like sunshine. Train the new shoots in as disciplined a way as possible, and these will fruit in the second year. After that, each autumn cut out some or even all of the branches that have fruited, allowing this summer's growth to fruit next summer. If you don't cut all out, some of those left will produce fruiting spurs again and again, resulting in a mighty tangle eventually.

Varieties: *Himalayan Giant* was once thought to be a cultivar of our wild blackberry but the credit probably goes to an American called Burbank who grew it in the 1880s, from vines sent to him from India, and gave it the name. In America now it's sometimes called the English blackberry, but it's a separate species, *R. procerus*, and just as wild, especially in Armenia where it comes from, and California, where they think of it in the same way we think of Japanese knotweed. Grow this type only if you have room to spare and want, in exchange for lots of luscious fruit, an annual battle with a very thorny plant that can put out wrist-thick stems thirty feet long in a season.

Bedford Giant is probably the one you might prefer, although it too can be over vigorous on good ground, or, where space is tight, *Merton Thornless*. There is only one variety of loganberry, since it's not really a species anyway, and that is the 1930s thornless mutation now known, as if it were a vintage car or a prisoner on Devil's Island, by the mystically figurative name of *LY654*.

STRAWBERRY, *FRAGARIA x ANANASSA*

Nothing can beat your own strawberries. As William Butler reportedly said around 1600, 'Doubtless God could have made a better berry, but doubtless God never did.' Had he had the duty of growing the berry, the learned Dr Butler might have wished that God had made them a little less of a bother.

The traditional way with strawberries is to have a cycle: new plants in the early autumn or the spring, pick off the flowers in the first summer, fruit the following year and the next and the next, replace with new. You get your new plants from allowing your best fruiting ones to throw out one runner each, at the end of which is a miniature plant that will grow ready for spring planting, if you help it by pinning it down – or, you can take it from its parent and pot it. Don't allow new plants in their first and so non-fruiting summer to have any runners. Snip them off. An alternative regime is to buy some new plants every year and plant them early, in June or July, and allow them to fruit the following summer.

If you have the so-called perpetual strawberries, they are planted in November to fruit the following late summer up to frost time. Dig up half your plants in March, split and replant, and do the other half next year.

In any case, if you have the flexibility, allow your bed to creep forwards, or backwards, as you follow your cycle, so that it is completely relocated every four years. This will help keep disease at bay.

Weeding is a pain unless you have spaced your plants widely, such as two feet each way, because of shallow rooting. You also should try to keep the berries off the ground, so they're less prone to rotting in wet weather and more difficult for slugs. A two-bird, one-stone way of doing this is to mulch generously all around your plants with sackloads of pine needles and other forest-floor autumn leaves. Strawberries are woodland plants originally and they appreciate the nutrients in leafmould.

Unfortunately you need rather more than one stone for your major predator, the dicky birds. You will need to net, almost certainly, and it may be worth making a bed-size frame of wood and half-inch wire mesh, like a small, low fruit cage. You could have the top in ordinary strawberry netting. The main thing is to avoid netting droop, which allows the birds to perch and peck through.

Another possibility for the really keen strawberrier is to borrow a technique from the PYO industry and build a strawberry cavity wall. It's not classical but we can't shut our minds entirely to new ideas, can we? Rather than growing in pots on the patio, make one very big, very long pot and grow in that. You are probably willing to get wood, hammer and nails to make your compost bins. Well, do the same thing in a long, thin shape and make your strawberries much easier to weed, harvest, protect and generally look after. Choose your own height and length of wall but make the cavity about a foot wide. Fill it with good compost, leaf mould, and muck if you can get it, and put a layer of sieved, weed-free soil on top. Put your plants closer together than you would otherwise, maybe just a hand's length apart, giving you enough room for watering, which you will need to do.

Varieties: among the best of the summer sorts for flavour is *Royal Sovereign*, but it's not the heaviest cropper and can get mildew. *Cambridge Favourite* is a popular choice and the benchmark against which newer types are measured. It's often involved in their progeniture, too. *Redgauntlet* and *Talisman* are excellent because they are high growers, naturally keeping their fruit up. *Talisman* has the better flavour but throws out runners like ticker tape, while *Redgauntlet* has bigger fruit and sometimes will give you a second flush later in the year.

Much cheaper and easier than a fruit cage, but will they be as effective?

RAWE CRAYME

... undecocted,* eaten with strawberys or hurtes** is a rurall mannes banket. I have known such bankettes hath put men in jeopardy of they lyves.

Andrew Boorde, 1490–1549. (*not boiled **whortleberries)

The older autumn/perpetual varieties such as *St Claude* seem to have disappeared entirely, so you pays your money and takes your choice among the new which, with the 'day-neutral' ones and a polytunnel, could turn you into a strawberry eater at Chinese New Year and at every solstice and equinox between now and Muckspreading Day. You can also buy, if you're really keen, wild strawberry seeds at about two quid a hundred.

All this about soft fruit has assumed you do not want to go to the expense and commitment of a fruit cage. If you already have a cage on your allotment, you're laughing. You could, if you wanted, turn your whole allotment into one big cage, but that would be going a bit far.

Currants and goosegogs are also highly suitable for the space-saving method of support and pruning called espalier or cordon, see below. If you're growing blackberries or logans, you're probably halfway there already. Such systems have much to commend them. They make harvesting easier and, generally, more plentiful; the fruit is easier to protect; winter washing of apples and pears is much more efficient. But, and it's quite a big but if you go by the Book of Grand Designs, there is a deal of intricate work involved.

APPLES, PEARS, PLUMS AND OTHER TREES IN TWO DIMENSIONS

Most allotmenteers would think that too much space is required, and possibly too much time to wait, to be growing trees that suck the ground dry of goodness and cast shadows where vegetable crops want sunshine. Certainly time is a consideration, but space need not be if you borrow from the walled gardeners of old and go for two-dimensional pruning and training. You can aspire to the classic shapes, of fans, candelabra, chevrons, the single-strand cordons that lean at forty-five degrees, and the ones usually called espaliers that have an upright middle stem with three or four pairs of wings going off to the sides, or you could design your own extravaganza, a fountain, say, or a big dipper, or the Hindu warrior goddess Durga, she of the ten arms.

Or, you could go with the flow and let the tree do the designing.

One of the very best dessert apples, Lord Lambourne, is a tip-bearer and so not suitable for espalier culture.

Another tip-bearer, pear Joséphine de Malines, is no good for espalier but so, so nice to eat.

The important matter is that you are restricting a plant's natural instinct, which is to grow onwards, upwards and outwards, by removing the option of outwards and restricting that of upwards. The first essential is a stout support, such as a wall, fence or specially constructed training posts and wires. You could, of course, use one side of your strawberry wall.

Next, you need forgiving plants that will bend to your will, so you need to get them young. Currants and gooseberries are ideal for 2D training; you start from scratch. With trees, you need to select a sapling that looks like it might fill the bill, such as any maiden (a one-season, single-stem whip), or, if you'd rather be there sooner, an older tree with likely looking branches coming off the stem at suitable intervals, or even one partly tutored already by the nursery.

Remember, there are two sorts of apples and pears in the world; some bear fruit on the ends of their shoots, some on little spurs that grow from said stems. It's the spur bearers you want. The tip bearers, some of which you would definitely consider for normal tree growing such as *Lord Lambourne*, *Worcester Pearmain* and *Blenheim Orange* apples, or the *Joséphine de Malines* pear, are no good for two dimensions. You would, on a fully trained espalier, only get eight fruit. Also check on fertility. Apples need a compatible companion for reliable fertilisation and some need two, and these need to have overlapping apple-blossom times. Pears also should not be alone, so choose varieties along those same lines.

Both have this curious thing called a chilling requirement, when they will not fruit unless, for hundreds of hours in the winter, they have experienced temperatures below 45°F (7°C), but pears need it not so much. They only require 600 hours, where apples need 900 minimum, and pears prefer a warmer summer thereafter, so please arrange for all this to happen in different parts of your allotment.

Pruning is the same as always, in winter, except you are only allowing upwards- and downwards-facing buds, not in- and out-facing ones. Cut off the top of the tree when it has reached the height you want. Abbreviate the strongest of this year's growths by half or more, deal more brutally with lesser youths, down to three buds, and altogether with anything pathetic. It's common sense, not quantum mechanics.

Stone fruit also are good for training but should not be pruned in winter. Look carefully for any damage or disease and prune accordingly. Some plums like *Victoria* are self-fertile, some need a companion or two for fertilisation, but all tend to do better with company.

SENT ONE DOZEN

... and one very fine Apricots from my best tree called the Anson* Apricot, to Mr. and Mrs. Custance at Weston House by my maid Betty. They sent us back some fine black Grapes which came from Mackay's Hot House, a Gardner at Norwich. August 24th, 1790.

James Woodforde, *The Diary of a Country Parson.*
(*Lord George Anson Anson, First Lord of the Admiralty and global circumnavigator)

Cherries want to be big and resent a lot of discipline, and so are not really suitable for espalier treatment nor, indeed, for an allotment. Some other stone fruit, such as peaches and nectarines, and apricots the most difficult of all, respond well to a 2D system in this country if they can face south or west in a long, warm, dry summer. That's not too much to ask, is it?

All your fruit trees and bushes (not strawberries) need a winter wash, mainly to kill over-wintering pests and their eggs. This spraying is done on dormant plants only. Any sign of growth and you're too late. You can also damage other plants nearby if they're in leaf, so a breezeless day is ideal. The traditional way, used for centuries, was with a tar-oil spray, marketed in more recent times as Mortegg, but that's now illegal and its replacement, called Growing Success and made of approved substances, is not as good. You need a lot of it because it doesn't linger on the bough, and it doesn't do for your woolly aphids. Still, it's much better than nothing. It's non-specific so it may kill friends as well as foes, but then so was tar wash and so are all such weapons of war.

Chapter Four

Cultivating And Fertilising
The Ground ... And Other Matters

Being organic and being traditional are not quite the same thing. Our ancient forebears had no choice but to be organic since there was no chemical industry and no remedies beyond what you could make yourself from the everyday things around you. Later, after scientific discoveries, gardeners generally used whatever they could to kill pests and

How do you turn this allotment in Derbyshire ...

into the same allotment in Derbyshire? The answer lies in the soil.

weeds. If effective chemicals were affordable they jolly well sprayed away, without knowing the consequences or even thinking there might be any.

For instance, a compound known as 'Paris Green' used to be mixed with bran to control leatherjackets. You put two ounces of this stuff, properly called copper acetoarsenite, $Cu(C_2H_3O_2)_2.3Cu(AsO_2)_2$, with two pounds of bran and enough water to dampen the mixture. You then spread it thinly on the ground; this amount would treat a fifth of an acre, roughly one thousand square yards or about four allotments. In a spray, the same compound was used against Colorado beetle and codling moth.

Paris Green had its name from its use as a rat poison in the Paris sewers. Since its introduction in the seventeenth century, this substance has been responsible for chronic illness and early death in countless artists, possibly including Cézanne and Monet, who used it to make a vivid emerald green paint. Among the other fatalities were those who wore clothes dyed with it and, we can assume, a goodly number of Victorian allotment holders. If you bumped up your Paris Green solution to be strong enough to kill certain pests, for instance gypsy moth, it tended also to kill the plants being sprayed and, presumably and eventually, even more of the people doing the spraying.

Lead arsenate, $Pb_5OH(AsO_4)_3$ or $PbHAsO_4$, largely took over as the insecticide of choice after about 1900, it being found more effective at lower concentrations. You could make your own lead arsenate by reacting soluble lead salts with sodium arsenate, or you could buy ready-made confections at the hardware shop or agricultural merchant's. It continued in use for years, even though it was known that residues stayed on the fruit and veg no matter how much you washed them, until after the Second World War when a miracle substitute was found: DDT.

Lead arsenate is now disused and/or banned pretty well everywhere although still classified by the International Organization for Standardization as ISO 765, a pesticide and growth inhibitor not requiring a recommended common name.

Hellebore, the dried, ground root of *Veratrum album*, has been used for thousands of years to kill lice and, by witches and incompetent herbalists, to kill people. Old gardening books freely recommend this highly toxic substance – '1oz fresh ground hellebore, 2oz flour, 3 gallons of water, well mixed, makes an excellent spray' – alongside lead arsenate, and one wonders how any allotment keeper lived to eat his produce.

ORGANIC (Chem)

Applied to a class of compound substances which naturally exist as constituents of organised bodies (animals or plants), or are formed from compounds which so exist.

The Shorter Oxford English Dictionary on Historical Principles, 1983.

Modern science has combined with common sense to tell us that many other marvellous treatments, whether to kill pests or weeds or to encourage growth, were at least as bad as they were good and so are best done without.

So if we're going organic, that is back to methods of cultivation used by those who had no access to marvellous treatments, no modern weapons with which to fight the gardener's enemies, are we not being a bit silly? Are there no benefits on the shelves of the garden centre?

As the immortal Kenneth Williams used to say, in the guise of Arthur Fallowfield on *Beyond our Ken*, 'I think the answer lies in the soil'. You on your allotment do not have acres and acres of it. You do not need to assure Messrs Birdseye that you will have a given number of tonnes of perfect, pest-free vegetables all ready to be harvested at a given time on a given day by machines as big as a house, and so you have no need of the aforesaid marvellous treatments required in such circumstances.

You can easily afford to go organic. It's not a big decision for you. So what if caterpillars try to turn your sprout plants into lace doilies? It's not the end of the world. Spray them with salt water. Pick them off and squash them. So what, if some of your baby cauliflower plants wilt and die because their little roots have been entirely consumed by the maggots of the cabbage root fly? You can afford to lose a few cauli plants. In any case, the high priests of the organic religion say that if you are pure in heart you won't get any caterpillars or maggots. Or something like that, which is almost true most of the time.

Definition of Organic

The first principle is to promote a nutritious soil full of the microscopic life that keeps it so. If the soil's good, your plants will be strong and healthy, productive and better able to resist all perils.

The second principle is all about natural balance. The existence of ladybirds supposes the existence of aphids as prey. In the past, the use of insecticides against – say – aphids also killed the ladybirds, and the aphids were better equipped to strike back, so more spray was necessary, and so on. In the balanced, natural world, ladybirds and aphids coexist in reasonable numbers without undue detriment to the allotment holder.

The third principle is diversity. Monoculture of any kind is bad. Growing the same things again and again in the same ground uses up the same narrow range of nutrients and provides pests with more and more encouragement. Crop rotation breaks the life cycles of those pests that specialise in certain types of plant and, because soil fertility works on a longer timescale than the gardener's annual calendar, rotation allows better development of the innumerable natural processes that go towards good living soil.

That, as it were, is the theology. What about the practice? Let's deal with the soil first, where the answer to everything lies. Organic allotment holders, those who do not want to have to go to confession, can use any amount of homemade compost, provided no fancy suspect starters have been used, and any amount of animal manure, provided they are happy with its origins. It should not, for instance, be the output of intensive farms. They can also bring seaweed on to the allotment, and certain naturally occurring minerals, to wit, lime, potash and phosphates made by grinding up rocks. Other traditional soil improvers are allowed, such as wood ash, hoof and horn meal and basic slag (limestone with phosphates absorbed during steel-making).

Compost

The basic idea of composting is to turn stuff that is no use into useful matter. Such an idea surely cannot imply spending large amounts of money on space-age composting equipment. You are transforming rubbish using the forces of nature. You do not need any help at all from the garden centre or the seed catalogue.

First, you must make your bin, a large double box, with solid walls to retain the heat of decomposition by aerobic bacteria and space beneath for the air to get in to make decomposition possible. It should be at least six feet or two metres long, more preferably, and three feet or a metre high, and divided in two. Both boxes thus made should have removable fronts. The idea is to make compost without needing to turn it, so plenty of aeration is essential. The floor of your boxes could be, for instance, wire mesh raised off the ground on a few bricks.

You should try and stick to a system of layers. Weeds, spent plants, grass clippings, household detritus, newspaper and so on doesn't always come in neat quantities sufficient to make a layer of twenty-two centimetres, or nine inches, but that has to be the plan. Between layers you should put sandwich fillings, in turn of wood ash, next layer, a sprinkle of lime, next layer, a little manure or chicken muck or, if you have a chamber pot in your shed, the contents thereof. Although rubbish will compost without such 'starters', it will work quicker with. If the stuff you are putting in does not include plants with soil on their roots, add a few handfuls of soil. When the first box is full, cover it with something to keep the rain off and start on the next one. With any luck, by the time that's full, the first lot will be ready.

Plot Planning and Crop Rotation

Most authorities will tell you to put aside part of your plot for the permanent stuff and then to divide the rest into three or four equal parts. The general rule is potatoes in one, brassicae and legumes in two, roots and onion family (alliums) and general in three, or, add a fourth for salads and general.

This allotment holder follows the conventional, Turnip Townsend style of rotation, moving the crops around bordered beds from year to year.

Or, potatoes in one, legumes and alliums in two, roots and general in three, brassicae and salads in four. These are very good plans if your requirements for different vegetables fit into equally sized rectangles. Certainly, some sort of crop rotation is essential, partly to prevent diseases of particular crops having the chance to multiply, and partly because different vegetables take different nutrients from the ground and want different nutrients put in.

If your soil is well cultivated and well supplied with compost, lime, comfrey, and manure if you can get it, the nutrient component of the plan assumes less importance unless you are looking for prize specimens or you need to extract the absolute maximum from the space.

It's a bit like those conundrums where you have five nationalities living in houses with different coloured doors, drinking different wines, eating different foods and liking different sorts of holiday, and you have to sort them out. The Norwegian likes claret and white-water rafting, the Italian lives next to the house with the green door, the person who goes mountaineering doesn't eat cabbage.

The fundamentals of rotation are:

- potatoes like lots of manure/compost
- root crops do not like recent manure/compost
- brassicae like lime
- legumes like lime
- potatoes do not like lime
- brassicae tend to leave a lot of litter behind, which protects and attracts slugs, making the next crop on that ground vulnerable
- the other stuff doesn't really matter much.

Your correspondent, rather than divide a plot into quarters or thirds, uses a rolling system, fairly inexact to be truthful, but more or less like this:

Season one: spuds and lots of muck and/or rich compost at the top of the plot, brassicae next to the spuds with lime, peas and beans next to the brassicae with a little lime, and roots at the bottom. Other stuff, including leeks, salads and so on, fit in wherever is convenient. Season two: spuds move to the bottom of the plot and everything else moves up one stage. Season three: up again, and so on. Season five is thus the same as Season one. This works, and allows a certain flexibility. Nobody grows exactly the same number of rows of everything year after year, and you might want to try something different, or more of this and less of that, so space can be allocated as you want rather than according to a predetermination. The main thing is to keep the lime lovers and haters, and the muck lovers and haters, far enough apart – if you can. If you can't, and you commit the venial sin one year of planting a row of potatoes where there is lime, you might get a bit of scab but the world isn't going to end.

ANIMAL MANURES

... are no longer easy to procure, but where they are, there is nothing better.
Encyclopaedia Britannica, circa 1935.

Cultivation – a non-digger's view

One of the many things you can do with a spade is pat a stray cat. Another very handy virtue of the spade is its noticeability as you wave it in friendly greeting to the children whose cricket ball has just landed on your cold frame.

Other than for such occasional uses, the spade need only be brought out for planting trees and for the annual lifting and sifting of some soil into the wheelbarrow to mix seed and potting compost.

Providing you have an allotment of a decent size and shape, you should hang up your spade and become the owner of a powered cultivator. Is it green to do so? Possibly not in the strictest sense but many might consider a few spoonfuls of petrol a good swap for hours of digging and years of back trouble, and it allows you to follow a system based on the common sense of the raised, well-ventilated bed without having to build any raised beds.

What is a decent size? The standard allotment of ten square perches is plenty. Anything above half that size would be big enough for you to become a lifetime member of the Rotavatarians, especially if it was a regular rectangle.

Why be an owner? The system depends on being able to use your powered cultivator whenever you want, for short periods or long, depending on the weather, your mood and inclination, the pressures of the season and so on. You really need to be an owner. It is impractical to hire, and borrowing so regularly would bring you round to co-ownership anyway.

What kind of cultivator? It doesn't really matter provided it's not a toy one. The system was developed by your

correspondent using a machine bought second-hand for £90 in 1983, which is still going strong. It was made by Flymo with a 3hp petrol engine. It has four four-prong digging things with a total width of just over thirty inches, which is about right for a triple row of onions or a double row of broad beans, and that is how the system came about.

By using the dragging anchor and your own strength to hold the machine back, it will dig down about a foot deep, meanwhile aerating and raising the soil. With a slim trench made by the central dragger, it will dig a fifteen-inch wide, raised bed of tilth on each side.

At the end of the row, you turn the machine and come back, digging along next to where you have just been, making another fifteen inches of raised bed, another slim trench in which you put your feet, and another fifteen inches. At this end of this row, you turn and return. See? Gradually you are making a series of thirty-inch wide, raised beds with narrow trenches in between. For maximum benefit from the sun, these raised bed-rows should run north–south.

The trenches made by the dragger are your garden paths. Only ever tread in the trenches. Never tread on the beds. If it means mincing down the paths placing one foot precisely in front of the other like a catwalk model, so what? Let them think what they like, while you think of all the digging you didn't have to do.

Of course, there is work before you get to this stage. In the autumn you will have puttered along, turning over whatever soil is clear of summer crops any old how. It doesn't matter about beds at this stage. Just go up and down once and across once, and again if you're enjoying it.

Come the last days of winter, when your thoughts turn to chitting seed potatoes, listen closely to the weather forecast. When a fine spell is upon you, barrow on your muck and/or compost and lime, in the designated areas, and turn it all over and in with your machine. Wait a week or two and machine it again. When you clear the last of the winter crops, do that bit too.

By this repeated cultivation you are combining the fertilisers and conditioners with the soil, you are aerating it all and breaking it up into the desired fine tilth without doing very much work. Also, you are exposing weed seeds to germinate and then be chopped off in their youth the next time you go over them, singing your happy cultivating song and thinking 'Got you, you little sods.' Ideally you want a dry spell after each machine session to wither away the weed seedlings. If it rains and thus replants them, you'll have to do it again. Doesn't matter. Only takes a few minutes.

Anyway, come the spring and you have made all or part of your plot into beds and trenches. Among the first things you'll put in are onions and shallots, and here's your first fringe benefit. The soft soil of the raised bed allows you to push your onion sets right in so the birds can't see them to pull them up. The little onions put anchor roots down, the green shoots appear above the soil and it's too late for our birdy friends. They'll just get cricks in their necks if they try. Over the season the bed sinks, revealing the burgeoning onion to the ripening sun.

You plant all your seeds and seedlings in the raised beds, except potatoes. For potatoes you wear your heaviest boots while driving your machine. Stamp your heel into the trench at foot or double-foot intervals as you chomp along, then walk back and place a seed spud in each depression. Stand in the next furrow and pull the soil over the potatoes with a hoe, so that you end up with a series of low ridge tents of soil, centred over the trenches, which have now-invisible rows of seed potatoes running down them.

This cultivation system worked well on clay soil in Suffolk although there it also needed a rake to get the beds into fine enough fettle. With sandy alluvial soil in Cumbria, the rake stood next to the spade in the shed, unused. Didn't need to do any raking. The big stones were chucked out by hand. The little ones could stay where they were. A dibber, a trowel, a hoe and a mechanical cultivator made the full set of equipment for planting.

You need a fork for harvesting, of course – potatoes, parsnips, leeks, and carrots sometimes – but you don't really need to own a spade. You could be the first person on your allotments to get a reputation for borrowing one.

PHILOSOPHY DUG DEEP

To own a bit of ground, to scratch it with a hoe, to plant seeds, and watch the renewal of life – this is the commonest delight of the race, the most satisfactory thing a man can do.

Charles Dudley Warner, a Victorian-age American, wrote these words in his book *My Summer in a Garden*. He was a well-known author, editor of Harper's Magazine and a collaborator with Mark Twain. He also wrote:

What a man needs in gardening is a cast-iron back, with a hinge in it.

Pests and Diseases

If following the high-church rules of The Soil Association, only three chemical weapons are allowed against pests: copper, soft soap and sulphur. Fungal diseases can be treated with formulae based on copper, such as Bordeaux mixture, or sulphur, and insects can be killed with soft soap but no longer with rotenone/derris as a last resort, because of a possible link with Parkinson's disease. Derris, a long-time natural friend to gardeners, is a friend no more.

The line adopted by EC directives also allows as insecticides and repellents azadirachtin, made from the seeds of the Asian neem tree; certain plant oils such as mint and pine; pyrethrin, made from a type of chrysanthemum; and quassia, extracted from a Brazilian shrub. Iron (III) orthophosphate can be used to kill slugs and snails. Only the Henry Doubleday Research Association mentions garlic, and surely there can't be anything non-OC (Organically Correct) with using tobacco and salt. Of course, no weed killers are permitted and they shouldn't be necessary on an allotment.

BRINE

Caterpillars do not like salt. Watering them with brine won't kill them but it can make them easier to see and dispatch by hand and foot. Slugs and snails also hate salt and, sprinkled on them dry, it will kill them. If you have friends who work on the gritter lorries or elsewhere in the council highways department, tell them a bag of rock salt would make an excellent birthday present.

FAIRY OIL

This will work against whitefly and other aphid-type pests. Make a mix of washing-up

IF YOU LIVE IN THE COUNTRY

... have vegetables gathered from the garden at an early hour, so that there is ample time to search for caterpillars, etc. These disagreeable additions need never make their appearance on table in cauliflowers or cabbages, if the vegetable in its raw state is allowed to soak in salt and water for an hour or so. Of course, if the vegetables are not brought in till the last moment this precaution cannot be taken.

Mrs Beeton's Cookery Book, 1930 New and Revised Edition

liquid and cooking oil, about a tablespoon of detergent to a quarter pint of oil. Add a dessertspoon of this to a quarter pint of warm water, shake and spray.

GARLIC AND CHILLI

As an insecticide spray, garlic is a broad range, persistent weapon, which means it (a) kills good as well as bad and (b) makes everything taste of garlic. Use carefully, don't soak the soil or you may be killing those friendly bacteria you've been striving to encourage, and don't do it near harvest time unless you like garlic a lot.

To make the spray, put about 4oz or 100g of garlic cloves in the blender with one pint or half a litre of water. Whizz to homogeneity. In a watering can or sprayer dissolve a knob of soft soap, or a squirt of washing-up liquid, in a gallon or five litres of water, the soap being to help the active ingredient stick. Strain your garlic soup into this through a fine sieve. Shake, rattle and roll.

As well as killing pests you can see, this spray may be a help against blight, potato and tomato.

If you had a very good crop of chilli you might try drying the pods and grinding them to a powder, for use against cabbage root fly. That which makes hot chillies hot, a substance called capsaicin, is widely touted as a cure for everything from cancer to hair loss but there is some empirical evidence that caterpillar-type beings also do not like it up 'em.

Rather than wait for your chilli crop to mature, you could buy some cheap chilli powder or the hottest curry powder from the oriental stores. Try dipping the roots of some of your brassica plants in it, or sprinkling it around the newly planted stems, and see if it makes a difference. Also unproved but worth trying is the addition of chilli to your garlic spray for use against caterpillars. Add a small handful of pods to your soup in the blender, or some powder.

HERBS

Said to repel rather than kill insect pests are quite a lot of herbs including hyssop, rosemary, sage, thyme, feverfew and rue. The method is to make up some strong herb tea. Fill a measuring vessel with the bruised or chopped leaves of herb or herbs, tip into a larger jug, fill the same measuring vessel with boiling water, tip on to the herbs when just off the boil, leave to mash. Dilute with one vesselful of cold water, add a squeeze of washing-up liquid, and there's your spray. Try it. Keep notes.

NICOTINE AND SOFT SOAP

This home-made insecticide was no problem in the days when everyone smoked. You just gathered up a pile of Woodbine and Park Drive fag ends, boiled them up, strained the brown sauce, mixed it with soap and diluted it with water and common sense. Nowadays you can't find fag ends except a few filter tips, so you will need to use some of your precious rolling tobacco. This mix should do for aphids, caterpillars, thrips, leaf hoppers and various other inimical bugs.

QUASSIA SOLUTION

The usual recipe is half a pound of quassia chips boiled in a gallon of water for two hours. The resulting liquid, with a few remnants of household soap dissolved in it, is used as a spray at one part to five of water. Finding quassia chips in cheap quantity seems not to be as easy as it was and the search may take you into some strange places, where headlice are hunted and love potions mixed. Quassia is good, or should we say very bad, for aphids and some caterpillars. It won't harm you at all, but it might make your salad greens taste slightly bitter if not very thoroughly washed or rained on.

SOOT

Slugs and snails don't like it and don't want to cross it when it's dry. Usefully also, it is a fertiliser and helps strengthen plants against attack.

... AND THE PESTS

Some of those pests specific to certain plants are dealt with in the text pertaining. Here we're talking about the most common and dangerous enemies.

Cabbage root fly: this pest presents a quandary for the organic allotmenteer. Good cultivation will help fight the fly by exposing the eggs and pupae to birds and by getting rid of brassica family weeds like wild mustard, and will strengthen the plants to resist, but only the time-consuming practice of making and placing little mats around the stems of every brassica plant will largely prevent it if it's common on your allotment

For this most goodly flower,
This blossom of fresh colour,
So Jupiter me succour,
She flourisheth new and new
In beauty and virtue.

John Skelton, 1460–1529,
The Commendations of Miss Jane Scrope.

site. There are no fail-safe natural treatments and there can be three generations in a summer, so the threat is there whenever you plant out a brassica.

Dipping each seedling's roots in soot or soot-and-lime mixture before planting may do some good. Growing your seedlings to a good size under glass, with plenty of room in the seed tray, will give them extra strength. A fine powder made of tiny ground-up fossils, called diatomaceous earth, is said to work by cutting into the maggots with microscopic sharp edges and dehydrating them, but if you're going to buy that you may as well buy nets and fleece. So, trust to luck or get out the scissors and a few bits of old carpet and make yourself some fly mats. They need to be about six inches across with a cut to the centre so you can place one about the stem of each plant.

Carrot fly: anti-submarine nets and ground-to-air missiles are only marginally less bother and expense than all the kit you could buy to defend yourself against this dreaded pest, whereas a careful sowing programme (see CARROT, page 70) and/or a few simple precautions can see you all right. The fly, which wants to lay its eggs beside your seedlings where leaves meet earth, hunts by smell and some of the old tricks are based on jamming the signals given out by carrot youth. These signals surge at thinning so try to do that in the late afternoon when the flies have gone home.

Planting onions and other strong-smelling plants among your carrots is one way but not an infallible one. It is probable that onions only give off a strong enough odour when they're a-growing; spring onions either side of your carrot rows should work to an extent. The same argument applies to garlic. Some herbs can act as deterrents; coriander is a convenient quick grower and, if the scent of battle lights your eye, you could put pot-planted rosemary, sage and members of the mint family upwind of your carrots on those sunny May days when the little swine is flying. On no account use parsley for this job; it will have the opposite effect.

Mixed sowings with marigolds is another measure but it rather puts a stop on the one really good natural method, which is to mulch your carrot rows with a goodly layer of lawn mowings. The decaying hay smell of dead grass puts the flies off. Fly predators such as centipedes like lurking beneath the mulch and mummy fly finds it harder to place her eggs properly in the hay. Meanwhile the mowings, like any mulch, are helping the young carrots develop their strength to resist. You can alternate this treatment with a mulch of wood-ash slurry, perhaps with some soot and lime mixed in, or put your grass clippings on top of wood ash. These treatments are not one-off. Repeat fortnightly in the fly season which, with global warming, could be practically any time although traditionally it is May/June and again in August.

All the old gardening books tell you to use naphthalene, the active ingredient of mothballs. Naphthalene is the subject of an EC ban and of a Risk Assessment Strategy by Defra, connected with the manufacture of grinding wheels. Mothballs are therefore illegal and if you were to find some at the back of a drawer and scatter them on your mowings mulch, you may well end up with unblemished carrots, but think of the guilt. Another way is to soak sand in paraffin and throw that about. Some say it makes the carrots taste of paraffin; others say it doesn't and, any road up, such a remote possibility is preferable to carrots tasting of nothing, as with commercial varieties.

Whatever measures you take, do not leave anything carroty lying around over winter to give sleeping quarters to carrot fly pupae.

Slugs and snails: there are almost as many preventatives for this serious, omnipresent garden enemy as there are gardeners. A fifty-fifty mixture of lime and soot might keep them away. If you have soot you will also have coal ash. Store it over a summer and add a few handfuls to your slug-preventative for extra potency. Aluminium sulphate, more usually associated these days with turning your hydrangeas blue, is a killer that will not harm your soil although not listed among the permitted substances. It will tend to make your soil more acid, so bear that in mind.

Traps are good. Bury jam jars so the beasts can fall in to the baited depths of cheap pale ale or lager, or place the jars side on, under something to keep the birds off, with bran or oatmeal inside, moistened with methylated spirits. The solid form of meths, used to power toy steam engines and camping stoves, sold as Meta tablets, when ground up and mixed with the bait seems to do well. Eat it and die, you slimy slugs.

They come out at night. You, a torch, a gardening glove, a pair of wellingtons and a carrier bag make a very effective weapon. The modern way is with nematodes – an application twice a year seems to be highly effective although no old-fashioned gardener would have heard of them. If you use them, don't also use garlic spray, which may well kill your nematodes.

These are battles. You should also have a general strategy for the war. Above all, as a permanent habit, try to give your plants a good start. Slugs are babykillers; they are less likely to mess with grown-ups. Keep your allotment tidy, clear the ground especially of brassica leaves, put all vegetable rubbish on the heap, don't give the repellent slimeys anywhere to hide, such as under old bits of wood or flat stones.

Encouraging natural predators basically involves making a pond, because you want frogs, toads and marsh flies. The larvae of these little brownish, yellowish, reddish flies, of which there are sixty-seven species native to Britain, eat slugs and snails.

Some birds also do that, but actively encouraging birds may be considered a doubtful practice by most allotment tillers. Compost heaps similarly are double edged. On the one hand they offer homely opportunities for slug predators such as ground and tiger beetles (*Carabidae*) – which also attack your aphids, wireworms, caterpillars and other pests – but slugs and snails breed there too. Compromise. Put your compost heap right over there, away from your growing beds.

FIVE A DAY

As already mentioned, it is hard for us today to imagine a diet almost free of vegetable matter. To illustrate just how things were, here are two menus, from the very top and bottom of society, and several hundred years apart.

Banquet menu, Coronation of Henry IV of England, 1399

Le primer cours
Braun en peuerarde *brawn with a vinegar, onion and cinnamon sauce*
Viaund Ryal *the royal meat dish was*
Teste de senglere enarme *boar's head rehorned, with*
Graund chare *spicy sauce*
Syngnettys *cygnets*
Capoun de haut grece *fat capons*
Fesaunte *pheasants*
Heroun *herons*
Crustade Lumbarde *cream and egg custard in a pastry tart, with prunes, dates, bone marrow and parsley*
Storieoun, graunt luces *sturgeon, with pike in a sauce*
A Sotelte Soltey *a fancy sculpture, mainly for show, possibly edible, possibly of sugar and pastry*

Le ij cours
Venyson en furmenty *venison stewed in a kind of milk pudding of wheat and sugar, served with*
Gely *a fruit jelly, possibly redcurrant*
Porcelle farce enforce *stuffed suckling pig*
Pokokkys *peacocks, roast and refeathered*
Cranys *cranes*
Venyson Roste *roast venison*
Conyng *rabbits*
Byttore *bitterns*
Pulle endore *Poulet d'oré – chicken made golden with saffron and egg*
Graunt tartez *vinegar sauce again, to go with*
Braun fryez *fried brawn*
Leche Lumbarde *pudding made with eggs, sweet wine, honey, dried fruit and bread, pressed and sliced*
A Sotelte *another sculpture, even fancier than the last*

Le iij cours
Blaundesorye *blancmange-style dish made with curd, chicken breast and almonds*
Quyncys in comfyte *preserved quinces*
Egretez *egrets*
Curlewys *curlews*

Pertryche *perch*
Pyionys *pigeons*
Quaylys *quails*
Snytys *snipes*
Smal byrdys *small birds, possibly larks and fieldfares, possibly in a pie*
Rabettys *more rabbit*
Pome dorreng *golden apples – pork meatballs dipped in a sweet almond batter and boiled in broth*
Braun blanke leche *brawn with almond milk, sliced*
Eyroun engele *eggs in jelly*
Frytourys *fritters – fruit in batter or deep-fried pastry*
Doucettys *small sweetmeats, the equivalent of petits fours*
Pety perneux *an early form of Scotch eggs, made with egg yolks, pastry and mincemeat*
Egle *yes, eagle*
Pottys of lylye *purple martagon (Turks' cap) and white madonna lilies were both common and the cooked bulbs were said to soothe*
A Sotelte *tadaaaah! The final sculpture*

Meals in a workhouse, Norfolk, 1794

	Breakfast	Dinner	Supper
Sunday	Bread, cheese, butter or treacle	Dumplins, meat, bread	Bread, cheese or butter
Monday	Same as Sunday	Broth, bread	Same as Sunday
Tuesday	Gruel, bread	Suet puddings	Same
Wednesday	Same as Sunday	Dumplins, milk broth or gruel	Same
Thursday	Same as Tuesday	Same as Sunday	Same
Friday	Same as Sunday	Same as Monday	Same
Saturday	Same as Tuesday	Bread, cheese or butter	Same

Chapter Five

Chick-Chick-Chick-Chick-Chicken

... lay a little egg for me.

> It shall be lawful for the occupier of any [allotment] land to keep, otherwise than by way of trade or business, hens or rabbits in any place on the land and to erect or place and maintain such buildings or structures on the land as reasonably necessary for that purpose.

So, says the 1950 Act, provided that the keeping thereof is not prejudicial to health, or a nuisance, and provided there is no bye-law against, you can have chicks and bunnies on your allotment. While your correspondent is fully versed in the art of shooting, paunching, skinning and cooking wild rabbits, he has no experience of rearing tame ones. In their admirable little book *Grassland Smallholding*, Doctors Bryce and Wagenaar have this to say about rabbits:

> The famed prolificacy of rabbits gives them appeal ... [and] ... they can be kept in wire-floored arks on grass during the growing season ... [but] ... a great deal of time needs to be spent in supervising the rabbits, especially when they are near to giving birth, so as to avoid losses at this time and ensure that the young are reared successfully.

The good doctors are really talking about rabbits as a commercial or semi-commercial enterprise and they conclude that the job's not worth doing unless you go for it entirely. You can't do that on your allotment anyway but if you have some spare grass and you only want a few bunnies for the pot, you might like to give it a try. Sources of breeding stock of meat-producing strains can be found on the internet, if you look carefully between all the websites that assume you are aching for a career in rabbit showbusiness.

Hens, on the other hand, need very little supervision provided you set things up properly. What does a hen need? No, she does not need a brand-new, architect-designed, luxury henhouse costing the same as three washing machines. A hen needs somewhere to roost safely in the hours of darkness, somewhere to lay her eggs, somewhere to shelter in filthy weather, somewhere to make a dust bath in hot weather, somewhere to scratch and potter about, and she needs food and water.

The place for roosting and sheltering can be the same, obviously, and the degrees of opulence and security are up to you. Perches for roosting in a hut should preferably be about three feet off the ground and they need not be anything special, so long as the hen feels she has a good grip on something stable. A highly polished and perfectly symmetrical hardwood dowel will not go down so well as a bit of old rough-sawn batten.

This hen-place should have some litter on the floor to absorb the huge amounts of hen-cack that will be dropped thereon. Straw is good, so are wood shavings and sawdust. Hay is not so good because it is usually full of seeds. Although the hens will get a lot of them, there will still be plenty to spring up when you spread the muck on your allotment. If you have a lawn at home, use the mowings.

An English game hen has no business in eggland, but business isn't everything.

This ark is well off the ground to allow birds to shelter and scratch beneath, also to avoid rats moving in.

The place needs a door for you to get in or at least reach in, and a hen's private entrance, which should be hen-sized, no bigger, and should be closable in the evening if there are foxes or other enemies about. As you will probably not be having chicks in here (see below) you won't have much trouble with the smaller predators, although crows will sometimes go in and take an egg, and so might a rat.

Somewhere to lay her eggs should be ... well, it doesn't matter much. They'll lay somewhere else anyway, some of them, but if you provide a couple of drawers out of an old kitchen unit, filled with hay or straw, fixed eighteen inches or two feet off the ground, most of the hens will mostly lay in most of them, most of the time.

Water is essential. You must supply it, and check it every day if it isn't naturally running. As to food, hens will get a certain amount on their own if they have the chance, but for good egg laying they need more, such as kitchen scraps cooked up in a mash, any cheap grain you can cadge, and layers' pellets, which have to be bought. The hens should be fed twice a day when laying, and once in the short days of December and January when they do not lay and spend most of their time on their perches. A good feed for ten hens is what you can get into a litre ice-cream tub.

Now, the most important facility of all: FREEDOM! Happy, healthy, untroublesome hens will have somewhere to scratch and doddle around. Officially, a free-range egg is one laid by a hen that has access to open air and vegetation-covered runs for half the time. She lives with no more than eight other hens per square metre indoors and has at least four square metres of space outside. Chickens raised for meat have less space.

Organic standards set by The Soil Association are better but the ordinary definition of 'free range' is a commercial and quasi-moral measurement, a face-saving compromise between the supermarkets and the welfarers. It has little connection with quality of hen life and hardly anything to do with freedom and/or ranging. Similarly, it has no bearing whatsoever on the quality of eggs.

While cooks in newspapers and on TV might tell you to use 'free-range eggs' in their recipes, the free-range egg in the supermarket looks and tastes – and behaves in cooking – the same as any other supermarket egg. It is no fresher. When you crack it, you get the same pale watery imitation of an egg. It came maybe months ago from a hen that only eats the same food as the battery hens and, largely, does not freely range. As one of a huge flock, she stays mostly in the barn because she just can't be bothered with her measly amount of Lebensraum. And, you are assuming that the egg is what its vendor says it is. Having seen fresh-egg sellers in market places reach for the battery stuff when the free range ran out, the point is made – not that egg sellers are dishonest, but that there is no discernable difference in the eggs except the price of hen welfare.

A small, movable run is handy for rehabilitating battery hens, and for directing their weed–seed picking, fertilising labours on to a particular bit of your allotment.

It is impossible to provide a hen with enough happiness-space and still produce eggs at a price that people will pay, which is why the only way to get such superb eggs in secure supply is from your own hens, or a very good friend. For example, the space per hen must be big enough to allow grass and general herbage to grow continually, to stay there and withstand the mess the hens want to make of it, and to provide breeding grounds for insects. If you cannot allot such space, you must somehow arrange things so that the space you do have is divided in two and the hens are let into it alternately, for a month or longer. The grass can recover in one part while the hens are scratching up the other part.

You can throw in plenty of greens, of course, from the allotment, which is a very good way of composting them and, as a result of this mixed diet, your eggs will be of an unparalleled excellence. The yolks will be a deep, deep yellow and rich in goodness, not because of dyes in the feed but because of the greens and the insects to feed on. The whites will be firm and strong in an egg beyond the wildest dreams of supermarkets.

Marrans, Warrens, or Buff Orpingtons?

There are many types of hen but only one costs the same as half a pound of butter, and that is a battery or barn hen that has been on laying duty for one year. The farmer replaces his caged flock at this stage with point-of-lay pullets, which form the next one-year shift to produce the one egg a day he expects in his centrally heated, twenty-four-hour-daylight egg factory.

He advertises his commercially spent hens in the local paper. If you buy ten of these hens, one or two will probably die and the rest will last another three or four years, not laying every day but laying more than enough for your needs. Surplus eggs from the high times you can put down in a crock or plastic bin containing a solution of waterglass. Waterglass, as your grandma knew, seals the shell and keeps the egg fresh. It's actually a solution of sodium metasilicate and you could always get it from your local chemist, and maybe you still can. It seems hard to find on the internet.

You half fill your vessel with solution as specified on the bottle it comes in, put it in a cool place, and pop your surplus eggs therein, making sure they are completely submerged. They will keep amazingly well for months but will not maintain their yolk-white integrity for poaching or frying. Scramble them, use them in cooking, make omelettes, but do not try boiling in their shells. The shells are no longer porous. The eggs will explode.

But, you say, did somebody intimate that rescue-hens might die? Your correspondent had one new hen from the battery farm that was so agoraphobic that it spent all its short life of freedom standing against a stone wall with its head in a chink. No matter how many times and with how much encouragement it was shown the brave new world, it went back to the wall, thrust its head in the hole, hid its eyes in the darkness, and waited

COCK-A-LEEKIE

In among myriad recipes, some fancied up with celery, cloves and figs, and onions – why would you want to put onions in cock-a-leekie? – the basis of this Scottish national dish can be found.

You want a chicken, obviously, ideally a boiling fowl or an old cock chicken that's had his day or, according to Scots folklore, the loser of a cockfight. Failing that, any chicken will do, such as that one on your allotment that has stopped laying. You want leeks, equally obviously, salt and pepper, and water. Strictly speaking, that's it. You put the chicken in a big pot, cover it with water, boil up, add the leeks, cook for hours, season, and serve in the manner of *pot-au-feu*, with the meat sliced and the leekie broth poured over, or serve the broth on its own and the meat as a main course with potatoes.

Or, you can add potatoes and barley to the cock-a-leekie to make it go further. Certain highly respectable lines of tradition specify the inclusion of prunes with the leeks, some cooks removing them before serving and some leaving them in.

for the grim reaper. Otherwise what usually happens is that a few might die for no apparent reason, and gradually the rest get used to freedom and the pursuit of happiness.

So, you go to the battery farm with a couple of jute or paper sacks, get your ten live hens for the price of two oven-ready supermarket 'chickens', and you put them in their roosting place for the first time at night. This is important. It must be at night, especially if there are other hens already there. Let them gradually find out about life outside, starting in the morning. After a few days, most of them will be more or less accustomed. They might go into moult and stop laying, but they'll come back in again. Don't worry about it.

These will be brown hens, very likely, probably a hybrid called Warren, because modern people like eggs to have brown shells and brown (and black) hens lay them whereas, years ago, people wanted white eggshells because they were purer and cleaner and somehow more, well, you know, like white bread. Also, because these Warrens are bred to be egg-laying machines, they have forgotten how to clock, how to sit on eggs for three weeks and hatch them, although they may start to go broody and sit for a while. They are not reliable, so if you do have a cock to make their eggs fertile, you also need an electric incubator or a mother hen. So, unless somebody gives you an incubator, don't bother with breeding at all. Buy some more cheap hens.

There is also the possibility of poulet au vin, or possibly murghi bhuna massalam. Free-range old boiling fowl are much, much better to eat than that weird meat substitute that in supermarkets is called chicken. If one of your old hens has given up laying or has become egg-bound (when you will see half-laid, half-made eggs protruding from her rear end), grab hold of her by her feet and hold her upside down with your weaker hand. She will go quiet. Take her by the neck with your stronger hand, head between first and middle fingers, and pull. You will feel the vertebrae separate and she is immediately and painlessly dead, if you have done it efficiently. Wings will flap and feet kick for a few seconds of nervous reaction. The rest is common sense.

That's everything about hens, then, apart from fleas and lice. Hens get little black fleas in warm weather and seem often to be hosting any amount of horrible moving specks of dull white. These don't do much harm to adult birds but they are very itchy on you and difficult to get off. All effective insecticides seem also to be birdicidal or organophosphates, and lindane has been banned, and permithrin is lethal for bees, cats and fish and may be carcinogenic, so what do we do? Keep the henhouse clean and don't overstock.

Chapter Six

Allotments Through the Year

APRIL

Early April in the greenhouse and everything's ready. Micky buys in his plants – Moneymaker and Gardener's Delight for tomatoes, and Telegraph for cucumbers, which will go in when it's a bit warmer.

Raspberries beginning to show. It's an old, large-fruited variety, name lost in the mists of time, to be cut right down each year. Micky is a big runner-bean grower; they'll be going in to the left of the rasps.

Cold weather and constant rain have put Micky well behind his usual work calendar.

A start's been made. With some decent weather, he'll soon catch up. The last of the purple-sprouting staggers on, with a few leeks.

MAY

Leek seeds ripening for next year, broad beans coming on, new potatoes, sprout and cabbage seedlings and some more ground made ready. Things are looking up.

Those rasps are really making up for lost time.

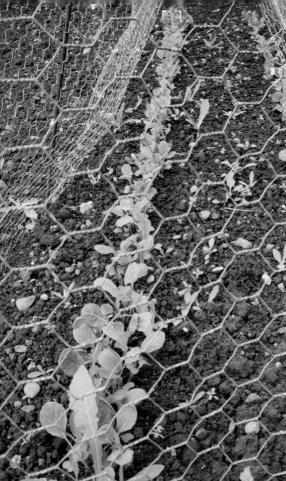

Brassica seedlings getting up to strength in Micky's seed bed.

Micky's no-nonsense scaffold shows his runner-bean intentions. In the background are sweet peas.

JUNE

How's that for a cucumber plant?
Up to the roof in a month.

Now the weather has warmed up, these
raspberries are racing away.

Broad beans ready to have their tops pinched out for a fine dish of early beany greens.

What a glorious sight. Yet more runners starting their climb, time to take the net off those dwarf peas, and the maincrop spuds well earthed up. With new potatoes elsewhere, Micky has planted his traditional variety for maincrop and winter storage, Desiree, a favourite in the east of the country because it can stand low rainfall. With a wet summer to come, this would prove to be a misfortune.

JULY

Micky and a couple of broccoli plants hide among the broad beans. Tops pinched and not a blackfly to be seen. The young bean pods are a-growing and some could be taken now to cook and eat whole.

You can't win 'em all. Sprout plants look terrible but will survive. A few Desiree were dug as new but then blight struck. By cutting off the foliage and burning it, Micky hopes to limit the damage.

Gardener's Delight are growing delightfully, with just a hint of blight in that yellowing leaf, to be removed and burned immediately.

A cabbage that somehow missed transplanting does well where it is, despite the caterpillars. Leeks and purple sprouting are ready to go out.

AUGUST

Micky lets his *Musselburgh* leek seedlings sit longer than some. He doesn't crop the leaves or the roots, and his leeks are as good as anybody's and better than most. The caterpillar damage next door helps to illustrate what a marvellous, pest-free veg is the leek.

Look, admire, and say 'I can do that.'

It happens. Despite every effort bar garden centre sprays, caterpillars did this to Micky's sprouts when he wasn't looking. Because they were such good, strong plants they will recover.

Brassicae struggle on despite pigeons and caterpillars, but blight has stopped potato growth in these maincrop rows and all leaves have been removed. Micky will leave the tubers in to harden their skins for keeping, hoping that the blight hasn't reached that far.

SEPTEMBER

Leeks in, late by some standards. Carrots suffering from early decimation by sparrows. Sprouts fully recovered from their cabbage-white attack.

—*Syringe Your Celery.* A rose-red solution of permanganate of potash should be used. Syringe without delay to protect from Leaf Spot disease, which in a few days can wither every leaf.

* * *

—*Plant Your New Strawberry Bed.* The plants should go in rich, deeply-dug soil. Set them 1ft. apart in rows 2ft. apart. September planting makes all the difference between a crop next year and sterility, or nearly so.

* * *

—*Remove Superfluous Strawberry Runners.* They weaken the parents and do little good themselves. When taking them up, cut off the old leaves from the old plants and burn them. Probably they are infested with Red Spider. In any case, they are living at the expense of next year's Strawberries.

* * *

—*Prune Your Raspberries.* You must cut off at the ground level all the fruited canes and burn them. Tie the suckers to the wires. If the suckers are numerous, reduce them to six.

That's the way to do it.

Broad beans left to go sare give Micky seed for next year.

OCTOBER

Chutney, anyone?
Green tomato and walnut jam is very good.

Look at those beauties. *Scarlet Emperor*
forever. He also has some white-flowered
The Czar in among the red, from years back.

Seems like a nice carrot.

Micky gathers some runner bean seeds. He does like runner beans.

NOVEMBER

And summer's lease hath all
too short a date.

Gardener's Delight still delighting in November but not enough warmth now to ripen them. They'll do it on the kitchen table.

The soil goes cold and everything stops. There are a few jobs to be done, perhaps tomorrow.

WINTER

Someone's going to very elaborate lengths about something or other. And that's a very fine raspberry system.

Pigeons are always a problem on this allotment.

Blackcurrant bushes on a Suffolk allotment, January 10th.

Most people like leeks, and they will stand any weather, but that looks like a lot, probably the whole seed packet. And they'll be sending up flower stalks in three months.

Test of a true allotmenteer: how do you feel looking at this picture?

The snow has gone and the celeriac still stands.

Broad beans *Aquadulce* in early February, with some early peas behind, protected from the pigeons.

Winter's almost over and the ever-faithful spinach beet is still trying hard.

Thanks, beetroot, for standing right through a hard winter. We do appreciate it.

Chapter Seven

You Are What You Grow

'A loaf of bread,' the Walrus said, 'Is what we chiefly need:
Pepper and vinegar besides are very good indeed.
Now if you're ready, Oysters dear, we can begin to feed.'

Lewis Carroll

So, what was, and still is, a healthy diet? What do we humans need to eat and drink to survive?

The walrus is a specialised feeder, delighting in bivalve molluscs, which it grubs up from the sea bed with its tusks. Perhaps a walrus on holiday might enjoy a dozen oysters but it would be most unlikely to find that particular type of bivalve at home, below the ice floes.

For the carpenter, the feast of oysters and bread would represent a fine meal, especially if he took a glass of milk with it and finished off with an apple, for it contains many of those substances we humans require if we are to maintain our physical integrity and not be absorbed into the environment. It's the same for every living thing: fuel must be taken in from outside to be converted into energy, body repairs (and growth in the young living thing) and whatever we need to keep us tickety-boo.

Some creatures, such as the oyster, have relatively simple needs. A few microscopic plants and animals, maybe some microbe-infested minutiae from a rotting corpse, and the oyster's internal systems can make what's needed. Humans are rather more manifold and need so many different bits and pieces to keep going that scientists cannot tell us everything about all of them yet.

Although we can digest and recycle much of that variegated fuel, we do need some things to be presented in a certain form or we can't deal with them. Some fuel components also are better suited to our recycling programme if they come in a certain form although we can manage them anyway if pushed. If we eat too much of some things, they can prevent proper use of other things.

If that were not difficulty enough, some essentials cannot be stored and so must be taken in regularly. For instance, without water we'd be dead in a fortnight, yet we could store enough fat for a year, to use as energy and insulation, and more and more of us seem to be doing that.

Most animals, except primates and guinea pigs, can make their own vitamin C out of glucose. As primates we can't, so without regular intake as children we have stunted growth, and/or later we get scurvy and die. We renew our entire skeleton every seven years (every two when a child), a process which relies on the element calcium. An average human has over a kilo of calcium in the body as a rule, mostly got from milk, dairy products such as yoghurt and cheese, also bread and hard water. Next time you have sardines on toast, eat the bones for the calcium. Another way is to eat tofu, sesame seeds and curly kale (er, pass the cheese, Louise). More complex still, to have a fully functioning calcium programme it helps if we also take in protein, magnesium,

phosphorus and vitamin D, and it hinders if we eat too much spinach and wholewheat matzo.

We can't take many of our essentials neat. We can't just grab a lump of limestone and eat that, and nobody would be keen on pure phosphorus, so we have to have them processed for us by other living things – plants, animals, bacteria.

We all know, or jolly well should know, that the human diet consists of protein, fat, carbohydrate, water, vitamins and minerals, plus the non-digestible transport provided by fibre. What most of us don't know is (for example) if we fail to have in our bodies something like eight thousandths of a gram of chromium, our insulin won't work properly and all manner of horrible things will happen. All we have to do to get our chromium is to eat a Weetabix or a wholewheat bread sandwich of meat or cheese and spicy pickle, and we're filling up on our fibre at the same time.

It is all so complicated and yet so easy. Lots of lots of essentials occur in lots and lots of foods. There are vitamins and minerals everywhere you look, on the allotment and in the food shops. If you eat fresh food in variety, a bit of whatever's on the go, you'll get what you need. Ah me and lackaday, there is no money to be made from telling people that.

If people got to know that all they have to do is pay regular visits to the allotment, the fishmonger, baker, dairy and butcher or their supermarket equivalents, and cook the stuff properly at home, what would happen to sales of diet books and magazines? Think of all the jobs to be lost if, for no better reason than not needing them, we stopped buying magic supplements. What would happen to the gurus? Oh no, not the gurus! Whatever would they do? And what about the food scares? Could newspapers exist without food scares?

Your correspondent's dearly beloved stands guard over her allotment.

Below are listed the main sources of vitamins and minerals – note, the main sources. Lots of foods have small amounts of various essentials and often you don't need much. Unless you have a medical condition, if you can't get enough magnesium in your diet it means you never eat any vegetables or fruit, and if you can't get enough phosphorus you never eat anything.

All vitamins and minerals are 'good for you', as are the foods that contain them. Shortage of any will cause trouble. Severe, long-term shortage of some, despite the amazing adaptability of the human body, will cause the ultimate malfunction.

Shortage of B2, for instance, will give you mouth sores. Shortage of B3, more usually called niacin, gives you pellagra, a very nasty ailment. Shortage of D gives you various bone diseases, and shortage of B12 causes pernicious anaemia. And so on.

This does not mean that more is better. Some of them are 'bad for you' if you have too much but this does not always make them poisonous. Nutritionists use the phrase 'balanced diet', which is a true but opaque way of putting it. What they mean is have a bit of everything and don't eat a great lot of any particular categories of food at the expense of others. For example, if you eat vast quantities of brown rice and other whole grains, you will increase your phytic acid to a point where your system precipitates vital elements – calcium, iron, magnesium – into insoluble salts. If you ate a polar bear's liver, it would give you a fatal overdose of vitamin A.

As one famous Australian cricketer said of another, 'His idea of a balanced diet is a cheeseburger in each hand.'

I want that strawberry over there, that one, no, not that one, that one.

Vitamins come in two main groups: those that are fat soluble and those that are water soluble. So that's how they come, dissolved in water or fat. All living cells have an amount of fat in them, so you don't have to eat lumps of fat if you don't like it.

WATER-SOLUBLE VITAMINS

Thiamine, B1: is found especially in pork, also in liver, kidney, yeast, cod roe, whole seeds – meaning cereals, legumes, nuts, rice and so on, kale, cauliflower, asparagus and milk.

Riboflavin, B2: milk (especially sheep's), dairy products, liver, kidney, yeast, egg, seeds and leafy greens. Here is your very own allotment E number. Riboflavin is known in another life as E101, a yellow/orange food colouring.

Niacin, B3: poultry and lean meat, dairy products, nuts, legumes, yeast, potato.

Pantothenic acid, B5: virtually all foods have some – the name means 'from everywhere'.

Pyridoxine, B6: yeast, liver, kidney, fish, jacket potato.

Biotin, B7 (also called H): meat, nuts, chocolate, vegetables, milk.

Folic acid, B9: widely found, chiefly in leafy vegetables, legumes, seeds, liver, yeast.

Cobalamin, B12: shellfish, fish, meat, milk and dairy products. This is the only vitamin with a metal atom (cobalt), and the only one completely unobtainable from your allotment unless you keep chickens. Eggs offer B12 but also block it to an extent. Chicken livers would be an excellent but possibly not sustainable source.

Ascorbic acid, C: blackcurrants, brassicae (especially raw), potatoes, most fruit and vegetables.

FAT-SOLUBLE VITAMINS

Retinol/Carotene, A: retinol is vitamin A from animal sources, especially liver and dairy. Carotene is vegetable A, in watercress, carrot, spinach, sweet potato, chilli, apricot, broccoli, tomato.

Ergocalciferol/Cholecalciferol, D: although occurring naturally only in animal products such as fish livers and oily fish generally, you can still get it on your allotment. Go out in the noonday sun with a reasonable proportion of your person exposed to the ultraviolet rays, and you won't need to take your teaspoonful of cod liver oil because your very own D factory will do the job. What's that noise? Ah, we hear the heavy-footed tread of the skincare police coming up the drive so, all right children, don't forget to slap yourself liberally with wossname.

Tocopherol, E: seeds are the thing, and leafy greens. Forget the almonds and avocado and think asparagus and cucumber.

Napthoquinone, K: eat your greens and you will get plenty of K. Menadione, K2, can be had from meat, eggs and milk but you will usually make it yourself with those friendly bacteria.

MINERAL SOURCES

Sodium: salt, sodium bicarbonate, therefore many manufactured foods.

Potassium: almost everything except fats, egg white, white bread, polished rice and tripe.

Sulphur: animal and vegetable proteins and the vitamin thiamine.

Calcium: milk and cheese, bread and baked products made with calcium-added flour; hard water.

Phosphorus: in all living tissues and most food.

Magnesium: in many foods, as it is an essential to chlorophyl and to oxidation enzymes in animals.

Iron: lost in sweat, urine, dead cells and especially menstrual bleeding. Iron is widely available in meat, shellfish, fortified flour, cocoa and other foods, but much is not absorbable. Seventy grams of prawns and five grams of curry powder contain enough iron for the day so you know what to order at the takeaway.

Oxalic acid (spinach, sorrel and rhubarb) and phytic acid (whole grains and pulses) precipitate calcium, iron and magnesium into insoluble salts. Too much phosphorus can prevent calcium absorption.

TRACE ELEMENTS AND THEIR ROLES

Cobalt: vitamin B12

Copper: enzymes, iron mobilising

Fluorine: tooth enamel

Iodine: thyroid, thyroxine

Manganese: enzymes

Molybdenum: iron and nucleoprotein metabolism

Zinc: enzymes

INORGANIC ELEMENTS IN THE AVERAGE ADULT HUMAN BODY, IN GRAMS

Calcium: 1050

Phosphorus: 700

Potassium: 245

Sulphur: 175

Chlorine: 105

Sodium: 105

Magnesium: 35

Iron: 2.8

Zinc: 2.5

Manganese: 0.21

Copper: 0.125

Iodine: 0.035

Chromium: 0.0075

EPITAPH FOR AN ALLOTMENTEER

What with all this enthusiasm and advice, we must remember that the pen is mightier than the sword. The effects of reading this book could be far greater than intended. We can easily imagine someone hooked on the pleasures of winning at the produce showbench, but what of that same someone who then takes addiction into the kitchen? Having grown the perfect vegetable, will there then be an unspoken but deadly serious competition across the allotments, to find the most obscure recipe from the least obvious source? Conversations at home might take an entirely new turn.

Him: What do you fancy for supper tonight, dearest heart?

Her: Dunno. What do you fancy?

Him: How about a pupton?

Her: A whatter?

Him: A pupton, my darling dear, my daisy flower, is a kind of terrine, or a pie without pastry, or a Scotch egg without the egg. The term apparently comes from the Latin word for doll, *pupa, pupae*, which came to be used as the scientific word for chrysalis, which is what a pupton can look like. It includes ... asparagus! Look ye upon my allotment asparagus and weep with joy, O ye who art beloved of me.

Her: Cool.

Him: I've had to adapt the recipe, which came from *Warne's Model Cookery* 1869, a bit, largely because I can't find a source of cocks' combs online. Althea, next door but one on the allotments, helpfully told me I can get them in France in tins.

Her: Who's Althea? Is she that fat one?

Him: Also the butcher looked at me in a funny way when I asked him to cut the soft palate from a calf's head. I bought some ox tongue instead. No need to buy the asparagus, of course.

Her: Ah.

Him: Anyway, I got the sweetbreads, and we already have some bacon and mushrooms in the fridge. And, prize of prizes, delight of delights, as already vouchsafed, I have brought home, in the best traditions of the hunter-gatherer, the first asparagus from my asparagus bed. At the allotment. The asparagus bed that I've been ...

Her: Do you want white or red?

Him: I'm just wondering whether to try and bone the pigeons, but if I just take the breast meat that will do. Have you seen this asparagus? Have you seen it? What do you think about that?

Her: I think red, don't you, with a pupton?

Some Useful Websites

www.brownenvelopeseeds.com
www.europotato.org
www.gardenorganic.org.uk
www.heritage-potatoes.co.uk
www.mammothonion.co.uk
www.nvsuk.org.uk (National Vegetable Society)
www.plantsforafuture.org.uk
www.realseeds.co.uk
www.rhs.org.uk/growyourown (Royal Horticultural Society)
www.suffolkherbs.com
www.thomasetty.co.uk
www.victoriananursery.co.uk
www.whyorganic.org

TO SECURE a good crop of vegetables, three things at least are necessary, viz., a suitable soil, pure seed and clean culture. The exposure for a vegetable-garden should be south or southeast, or nearly so. The soil should be naturally rich and friable, a sandy loam being about the best. If the soil be stiff, it should be gradually mellowed by the free use of barnyard manure, or, if convenient, by the addition of sand. If wet, or inclined to hold an excess of moisture, it should be underdrained, preferably by tile; but, if possible, a location should be selected naturally dry and free from surface water.

A dark-colored soil, or one supplied with a goodly portion of decayed vegetable matter, will produce the earliest crops. If the soil be shallow, it should be deepened gradually by plowing or spading an inch or two deeper each year, and not all at once by trenching or subsoiling, unless manure and money both be abundant. A sandy soil may be greatly improved by adding vegetable mold from the woods.

Another Thorburn wrote this in 1821, since when approximately 257 squillion gardening books have been published. The basic truths and tenets remain the same.